# I'm Tired & I Need a Nap

## A TACTICAL SURVIVAL GUIDE FOR NEW AND EXPECTING PARENTS

# MARIE S. HERDER

WESTBOW
PRESS®
A DIVISION OF THOMAS NELSON
& ZONDERVAN

WestBow Press books may be ordered through booksellers or by contacting:

WestBow Press
A Division of Thomas Nelson & Zondervan
1663 Liberty Drive
Bloomington, IN 47403
www.westbowpress.com
1 (866) 928-1240

Because of the dynamic nature of the Internet, any web addresses or
links contained in this book may have changed since publication and
may no longer be valid. The views expressed in this work are solely those
of the author and do not necessarily reflect the views of the publisher,
and the publisher hereby disclaims any responsibility for them.

Any people depicted in stock imagery provided by Thinkstock are
models, and such images are being used for illustrative purposes only.
Certain stock imagery © Thinkstock.

ISBN: 978-1-5127-7657-7 (sc)
ISBN: 978-1-5127-7659-1 (hc)
ISBN: 978-1-5127-7658-4 (e)

Library of Congress Control Number: 2017902935

Print information available on the last page.

WestBow Press rev. date: 03/10/2017

# Introduction

More than any other thought over the past few years, when someone has encouraged me to write a book, there is one thought that floats to the surface. It's simply this, "I have no advice for anyone on how to live. I only have stories of survival."

I can't write a "how to" book that would be placed in the self-help section of Barnes and Noble.

I can't write a book about faith, as it seems that everything, absolutely EVERYTHING I know is still a learning process and a work in progress. There have been a few times in life when I had the audacity to think, "I've GOT it!" It's at that exact moment that the 'it' changes and goes deeper, and I realize that I was only still just scratching the surface.

I can write beautiful lines about my children and my gratitude that they're in my life. I can bring tears to an audience with the adoration I have for them and the absolutely overwhelming sentiments that sometimes well up from within. But I can't tell someone how to mother. I can't give them a manual for life. Every child is different, even my own. And on different days, they're different people. What worked one day will not work the next. What soothes one soul, makes another little soul question. When it comes to "mom-ing," I can only honestly say that I'm thankful my children are surviving it. I haven't lost one... Yet. And what kind of title would that EVER be on a shelf about successful parenting?

If there was a section that I could conquer, or an area of expertise I could dominate, I'd like to think it would be just this: honesty. Sugar coating aside, life is difficult. At best, life is messy. And while it's flattering to think that I may have something to offer the world, I recognize that's only an illusion. I only have stories of days that have slipped into nights, and months into years. Life is vibrant at times, horrendously monotonous on others. One day builds onto the next, and miraculously we're all still here.

For that, I find myself grateful.

One more boy was just delivered to us this summer. That makes four, and I still can't say with certainty that I know what I'm doing. I've put together the best of the stories that have shaped our world since my husband and I married. These stories shed light onto our daily grind. Sometimes that light is too bright, and it illuminates the things that most families would rather keep hidden. There are a lot of times during parenting that I've spent with the proverbial palm of my hand over my eyes. There are a lot of times as a mom that I've felt like a failure. I share these stories to give mommas and daddies around the world hope, and to let them know that they aren't alone.

For the record, I've also let my children go through these stories to ensure that they don't feel as though the sharing of these memories in book-form will land them in counseling sessions as adults. For the most part, they approve of this compilation. Perhaps only cheap therapy will be needed later in life. Enjoy!

First off, I want to make a few introductions. You need to become affiliated with the members of our unit. Welcome to our chaos! At any time, you can snap this book shut and walk away. I don't have that option, so I'll just be patiently wait for you to return and keep me company. Sometimes it's lonely as one of the few sane people left on the planet. It's good to remind myself sometimes as a parent, that others survive the insanity! Now, without further ado, please meet the squad. Please note that names have been changed to protect the privacy of our kiddos.

I'm married to The Gentle Grizzly or, The Griz for short. He's my best friend, and battle buddy. I'd take a bullet for him. Oh, I'd complain about the pain afterwards. I'd torment him through my healing time. I'd definitely demand several breakfasts in bed, but I'd take a bullet for that man. We've been through a great deal together in what seems to be such a brief time. While there has been a LOT of laughter, there have also been tears. He's a good father, and he's following in the footsteps of our Father. I honestly can't ask for more than that.

Brief background on our crazy family: When The Griz and I met, we were both already plus one. He has a daughter who doesn't live with us, but we see her as often as we can. She's beautiful and full of life and laughter. She loves her sister and brothers deeply, and she's brought joy into our lives. I'm thankful for having the chance to get to know her. She makes a brief appearance in some of these tales during her summertime visits to our home. For the sake of her anonymity, henceforth she'll be known as Shy. It's only appropriate. She's hesitant to allow people close, but when she does... Her heart is golden.

My plus one was only barely walking when The Griz and I met. He's been the only dad she's ever really known. He stepped up and has loved her and protected her fiercely since just after her first birthday. Hazel eyed and freckled, she's growing too fast into adult beauty, meet The Barb or B-Dubya, our information station, who ALMOST knows the facts to everything. We call her our household reporter. While she's now entering her adolescent years, and she's trying hard to learn her way as a civilized human, as she's not always been a proper lady. She's a firecracker with an imagination the size of Texas and a compassionate heart. She's a story teller too and has been since she was in diapers. She's always appreciated the thrill of a good audience. When she goes to spend the night with friends, I have to pray that none of her tales cause our family to end up on the local nightly news.

Squad member #4 is a special kind of a character. You see, while The Griz and I were beginning our honeymoon, the sickness started. Nine months later... Meet Captain A. Caramel skin and deep brown eyes, he's got me wrapped around his finger, although I would NEVER admit that to him. He's my middle kid for sure. He's always game to remind us of the things in life that aren't fair, and he's our strong-willed soldier. He's tough as nails one minute, and the most empathetic of our three kids the next. He takes everything in, and digests it. He sees the world in vivid colors and doesn't miss much. He remembers everything, except how to turn off lights and clear the table after dinner. He lives fiercely, loves hard, and soaks up every single minute. He's our resident skeptic, and needs to test things out before fully committing himself. He's the loudest when he's injured, the most active when he's tired, and the most vocal about … well… everything.

Next in line is my blue-eyed thief of hearts. Meet Squad member #5, aka The Honey Badger. He's every bit of every stereotype about the baby of the family. He hasn't relinquished that title yet to our youngest, who was only born a few months ago. He's rowdy. He's 100% boy. He's mischievous. He's carefree. He's a total dictator, although he doesn't realize even at four years old, that he's too little for his opinion to count for much. We remind him occasionally that until he masters the art of not eating things off the floor, his mandates and opinions are invalid. He's been dubbed "The Honey Badger" with good reason. In his overwhelming curiosity, he's had the uncanny ability to dismantle and destroy everything he's touched since he arrived on the planet. He doesn't really care about anything at all except what is happening in his world at any particular moment, and all things sugar related. He's a candy-o-holic, and he's shameless. He's not afraid of anything, with the exception of large dogs. Given the opportunity, he'd take on the devil and all those flames with a water pistol.

Bringing up the tail end of our family unit is our newest addition. He's been here only long enough to earn the name Pumba. From the pompadour on his head to the green exclamations from his nether regions, he has won the title of Pumba. My lil' stinker. He's a night hound, and due to this one fact, I've called him PLENTY of names in the short time he's been here, but nothing proper. His personality is only just beginning to develop. He's got personality traits of both Captain A and the Honey Badger. When he's angry, he's angry to his CORE! When he's happy, it lights up the whole house. He has been absolutely ESSENTIAL to this whole editing process. I'm convinced that if one has never had the "pleasure" of editing a book while a baby is yelling at them and barfing on their shoulder, then one has never truly lived. Pumba is our last addition, unless we decide to go the route of adoption. I'm soaking up every minute... Every single minute... Every single after midnight minute that he demands to spend with this bleary-eyed zombie-momma... this zombma.

These are totally different kids, who bring totally different issues to our table on any given day. They have totally different personalities, and they keep us on our toes and keep us up at night. These kids make me realize that while parenting is beautiful, it's also a battleground. There are MANY days where after tucking them in at night, I feel like a success simply because we're all still breathing.

Where ever you are on your parenting walk, remember one thing. If this squad can survive it, you can make it! You'll be bumped and bruised. You may come out with battle scars. You may end some days looking more like roadkill and less like a human, but you'll make it. We all do.

Throughout this book, I'll be sharing with you some tips that have helped us survive. There will also be stories of things that you should never EVER do as a parent. Those are the PRO-parenting experienced tips. These are the "I've learned by fire so that you don't have to" moments. Study our mistakes CAREFULLY!

With all of that said... Welcome to our world.

~~~ ★ ~~~

Parenting Survival Tip # 1: You'll just have to suck it up and explain things you thought you'd never have to tell a reasonable person. Kids. Aren't. Reasonable.

That moment... When you see your five-year-old karate side kick the bathroom door to open it to go potty. As this is happening, you hear your husband say, "SERIOUSLY?"

And you have to slowly proceed down the hall and disappear to keep from laughing while your husband teaches the child that one should use their hands to open doors.

#LifeWithBoys
#HeAintGonnaMakeIt
#CaughtHimHangingFromATowelRackYesterday
#WeHaveThreeOfThem
#IAintGonnaMakeItEither

~~~ ★ ~~~

Parenting Survival Tip # 2: Always... ALWAYS spell the good stuff. It makes it more desirable.

Captain A: [whispering] Momma... Are we gonna get some T- E- R- R- O- S- N?
Me: What?
Captain A: [insistent] Are we gonna get some T- E- R- R- O- S- N?
Me: What is that?
Captain A: Some chicken wings. I need some.

~~~ ★ ~~~

Parenting Survival Tip # 3: Don't ask questions. You really *REALLY* don't want to know.

Captain A: (holding up his left index finger) This is my favorite finger. The finger nail doesn't even grow. So, I never have to cut it. It's my best. I don't even pick my nose with this finger. I use the other one.

~~~ ★ ~~~

Parenting Survival Tip # 4: Let them imagine. Life will drain them of creativity if you allow it.

The kids are cutting and couponing in the kitchen floor. B-Dubya wants the vacuum for $79.00. Captain A has his heart set on a magnet dry erase calendar and a set of seat covers for a car. And for daddy... Captain A picked out some $.99 shirts and a multi-tool combo. I'm fairly certain that the Honey Badger just requested to buy a Cyclops I think.

Suuuch a productive shopping session...

~~~ ★ ~~~

# Day 1

A memory from April 2010:

I asked my daughter tonight what she learned about in class.

"About the woods," she stated.

She then got really specific, going on to add emphatically, "Do *not*, [pausing for dramatic effect] go by yourself in the woods. Do *not* touch everything in the woods you see. There's stuff out there that makes you itch."

She gave such wisdom, so much great advice.

"Do *not*," she emphasized, "stuff berries in your pockets and eat them when your parents aren't looking. It's *not* cute. It's *not* safe."

Thanks dear. That's good. I was so tempted, but now I won't be stuffing berries in my pockets.

"Do *not*," she continued very gravely. "Eat any berries at all in the woods. Unless your mommy packed you a picnic lunch. Then it's okay. But berries from the woods can make you barf."

What is it with the berries?! Ok, Okefenokee Joe, I get it!

"Do *not*," my little Eagle Scout continued, "take your knife out and write on the trees. It's not cute. And it will kill the trees. Find another way to mark your path. Don't cut the trees. God created them. Don't kill them Mom."

I put down my pocket knife. I stopped carving my initials. There was such depth from a four-year-old. She was gravely serious. I mean, there was nothing more important than saving the trees at that moment.

She's amazing. Someone had taught her a life lesson, and she shared it. B-Dubya knows it all. She's so self-assured in her "rightness," I won't even correct her sometimes. It's good to see her passion and to take notes on how to survive life.

This four-year-old is so amazingly in touch with all the ins and outs of daily existence. She speaks with such passion. I don't even mind that she thinks a big oil-run rig that plows dirt is called a bull dumpster. I also don't mind that this little person who thinks she knows so much is still convinced that invisible alligators live under her bed. It's part of the fun of imagination.

I don't mind that she's my miniature portrait, with crazy curly top hair and a laugh to die for.

I don't even really mind that she thinks farts are funny, although I don't encourage this behavior. It's actually rather annoying, but then I stop and think she's only got such a short time to be a kid. I can't force myself to "proper-ize" her while she's still in the midst of the magical years. The time will come for pantyhose and heels. The time will come for only laughing politely over tea and swapping recipes at the work lunch table. The time will come when life will hit, and she'll be forced to grow up.

May those days be a lifetime away. I want to cherish her laugh while it still chimes around corners. I want to hear her dreams. I want to go to work and always find a randomly placed, stuffed blue bear in my bag, "to remind me not to forget her." As if I could forget the hours of labor and the wretchedness of childbirth! How could I ever not remember the months of morning sickness? And one can never just get over the sharp little puppy dogs that I sometimes stepped on when trying to get to her bedside as she had a bad dream. No sweet child, I could never forget her.

I can't help but think how silly I still must sound to my parents.

"My children will never_____." You fill in the blank. Oh, how my parents must chuckle! I bet when they were raising me, they never anticipated their baby having a child out of wedlock and a broken heart. They never saw that curve ball coming. No one can prepare for that.

"I'm going to retire young and enjoy my family." I've said that. Oh, the sighs my parents must have swallowed. I bet they'd had the same dreams once.

I wonder if the magic of a happy spirit ever wears off. Does my mom still look at me with a contented smile when I say something that she knows will never happen? Does it still matter that I believe in miracles? Does the magic of childhood ever completely dissipate? Will I always be someone's baby? In the eyes of my parents, will I always be the little knucklehead who caught my own hair on fire by sitting too close to the flames on a chilly Sunday morning?

Will my daughter always be the most amazing little scientist I know?

How does my rambling spirit sound to my Creator? Does He look on my temper tantrums and want to throttle the life out of me some days? Does He give an exasperated sigh when I question His motives again for the $457,654,234^{th}$ time this year?

Does "I'm sorry" ever get old to Him?

Will I always be His child?

I look at the magic of my children, and I can't ever imagine saying, "Not this time. You've gone too far. I don't love you anymore." I don't know that I could ever get to that point, but perhaps that too is dream and whimsy.

I stare at them gently sleeping, and I can't fathom ever thinking that they pressed too hard. This time, they shouldn't come home, they've done too much. I can't forgive this.

I stare at my cluttered home, and my dirty dishes, and the mounds of laundry, the toothpaste clump in the guest bathroom floor, and the smeared nose prints on my back window, and I can't grasp ever being so hurt by them that I wouldn't want them over again for Sunday dinner.

My kids aren't perfect. They're kids. They're sometimes obnoxious. They're flawed. They're selfish. They're hopelessly relentless. And they're mine.

And I'm His.

And I'm flawed, and broken, and bent, and perfectly imperfect in my brokenness.

I'm thankful, that the same God who loves a little girl and her bull dumpsters, calls me His own. He watches over both of us. His arm is long enough to reach us in our most broken places. I can't ask for more than that. And I can't aspire to be a better parent than the example that I see set before me in my heavenly Father.

She's still staring hard, making sure I received all of her four-year-old wisdom. My eyes connect to hers, and I make the vow and promise her: I'm not stuffing any berries in my pockets to snack on later.

Mental note taken.

~~~ ★ ~~~

Parenting Survival Tip # 5: Don't choke.

For future reference, if you ever choke on your breakfast while the four-year-old is in the room, expect to die. Expect no sympathy. And be prepared to answer thirty-six questions about why you're choking as you slowly asphyxiate.

~~~ ★ ~~~

Parenting Survival Tip # 6: Encourage them to notice differences...
and appreciate them.

B-Dubya: You're caramel.

Captain A: Ummmm... No, I'm not. Daddy is chocolate. I'm
chocolate too.

B-Dubya: No. You're caramel.

Captain A: (angrily now) I'm *chocolate* like my DAAADDYYYYY!

B-Dubya: Ok! Ok! You can be chocolate. I'm cookies and cream...
With swirls. Mommy, can Honey Badger be vanilla like you?

Captain A: You're rainbow swirls B-Dubya. I'm brooooown
chocolate.

I'm content today, blessed beyond measure. While these incredible
kids see in color, they don't see anything but flavors to be proud of.

~~~ ★ ~~~

Parenting Survival Tip # 7: It's not okay to interrupt.

Captain A: Father God, thank you for this day that you have
given. And please don't let there be any tornadoes or bad
weather. And please help Faith to come over tomorrow. And
please help Honey Badger to turn two and then three and four
and five and six and seven and eight and nine and ten and
eleven and twelve and fourteen and sixteen and eighteen and
twenty-one and twenty-three and twenty-seven and thirty
and thirty-three and thirty-four and thirty-five and thirty-six
and thirty-seven.

Me: (interrupting for the sake of time) Son, please continue praying. Don't get sidetracked.

Captain A: (pausing... he's definitely offended) That *was* my prayer.

Me: (quiet... without interrupting again. I stand corrected.)

Captain A: (continuing past my rudeness) And Father God, let him be thirty-nine and forty and thirteen and fourteen and fifteen and sixteen and nineteen and twenty-three and twenty-seven. And then let him be bigger and bigger and bigger and bigger and bigger. And help him not to be mean to me. And help B-Dubya not to be ugly and mean to me. And help mommy to be not mean to me. And tomorrow can it please be supper first... Then lunchtime... and then breakfast last? And please don't let there be any bad weather or tornadoes on Mother's Day. And Amen.

~~~ ★ ~~~

Parenting Survival Tip # 8: Oldies can be goodies.

Just overheard my daughter, "Goooooooooo Kevin! You can do it!" A few seconds later, "Come on Grandma! You've got this!" And then, "Do it Joyce! I know you can!"

*The Price Is Right*... Teaching children everywhere to encourage the masses.

~~~ ★ ~~~

Parenting Survival Tip # 9: Know their terminology. It's imperative to figuring out what the in the world they're talking about.

Captain A: You know Mom. You know that green guy? The one
   with the green nickels? Him Momma...
Me: (recognizing immediately that 'nickels' are the body part
   located on a man's chest) Are you talking about the Hulk son?
Captain A: Yeah. Him.

~~~ ★ ~~~

Parenting Survival Tip # 10: Celebrate the small victories.

That moment... When you sanitize your son's hands, and then
you observe him immediately picking his nose.

Well... At least his left nostril is bacteria free.

~~~ ★ ~~~

Parenting Survival Tip # 11: Encourage them to think outside
the box.

B-Dubya: (yelling from the back seat) Roadkill! Awesome! It was
   a dead deer... Or maybe... Ummmm... It could have been a
   squirrel.

~~~ ★ ~~~

Parenting Survival Tip # 12: Remind yourself often that you're
doing the best you can. You're not a failure. It's not you. It's them.

You'll have to research things you never dreamed for your
"angels."

I just Bing searched "my kid drank pee water." It made me feel better as human when over thirty-one million hits came up as a result of my search.

P.S. *Don't* ask me how my night went... I'm going to bed.

~~~ ★ ~~~

Parenting Survival Tip # 13: Be careful what you say out loud. They hear EVERYTHING!

B-Dubya: Ooooooh Momma!!! Look... An exercise program for you!!!! It's only $29.00.
Me: Did you just call me fat?
B-Dubya: Noooooooo! I have just heard you talk about exercising and losing a few pounds.
Captain A: (ever the realist and master of jumping into conversations where nobody even asked him) Yes, Momma. She said that.

~~~ ★ ~~~

Parenting Survival Tip # 3: Don't ask questions. You really *REALLY* don't want to know.

While Captain A is doing his chores and putting away the silverware, I politely inquire:

Me: Son.... Just out of curiosity... Have you picked your nose today?
Captain A: (completely avoiding the question) Why? Is my nose bleeding?

Me: Ummm... No. It's not bleeding. But son... Have you picked your nose today?

Captain A: (matter-of-factly) Yes.

Me: (wanting to make a point so that he remembers for next time) Son... Have you washed your hands today?

Captain A: Ummmm... No.

Me: How do you know that there aren't boogers on all of the clean silverware then?

Captain A: (without blinking) Because I ate all of them. You're safe.

#FacePalm
#ParentingFail
#WhyDidIAsk
#BoysAreDisgusting
#IQuit

~~~ ★ ~~~

Parenting Survival Tip # 14: Sometimes, it pays to just sit back and watch.

Down the hall, I hear:

(knock knock knock)

B-Dubya: What's the password?

Captain A: (confidently) Giraffe.

B-Dubya: No. This is the mermaid room. The password is "mer-friends." Say it.

Captain A: (trying to avoid humiliation) Smurf-ends.

B-Dubya: No. You heard me. Mer-friends. Say it.

Captain A: (mumbling quietly) Mer-friends.

B-Dubya: (thrilled, she snatches the door open) Excellent!!! Now. Say the whole thing... Or I won't ever let you in. I'm closing the door. Try it again.

(knock knock knock)

B-Dubya: (in her most chipper, sing-songy obnoxious voice) Whooooooo's thereeeeee?

Captain A: (a deep sigh... dejectedly and ashamedly under his breath) I cross my heart of the mermaids. The password is mer-friends.

The door opens, and he slinks in.

It appears as though my son just sold his soul to the devil.

~~~ ★ ~~~

Parenting Survival Tip # 15: Encourage them to try new things... Then grab your camera.

Just totally convinced B-Dubya it was great idea to attempt sledding down the stairs on a pillowcase. I wouldn't exactly call that first run successful... But it was DEFINITELY entertaining for Captain A and I.

#EpicParenting

~~~ ★ ~~~

Parenting Survival Tip # 16: Instigate play time. Encourage laughter. Stir up a little trouble. It's worth it when they know they can play with their parents.

Captain A: (carefully instructing big sister) No. Stop! Act like you don't know me! I'm Superman. You don't know me. I'll be in your closet. You don't know me.

B-Dubya: Okay. Go hide.

Me: (probably stirring up unnecessary trouble) If there was a man in my closet that I didn't know… B-Dubya, I wouldn't be very nice to him. In fact, he'd probably get shot.

B-Dubya: OHHHHH! Good idea. Where's the rubber band gun?

Captain A: (silent… unsuspecting… in the closet…waiting)

The door opens.

B-Dubya: OHHHH! There's a strange man in my closet. And he's Mexican!

Captain A: (not even phased by his sister's antagonism)
    I'M NOT MEXICAAAAAAAAAN. I'M SUUUUUUUUPERMAN!!!!

~~~ ★ ~~~

# Day 2

We got home last night, after a looooong day. My daughter had been semi-pleasant (despite the fact she'd had no nap). As we were pulling in the driveway, she started to whine. All I could think was, "Her bed is only a few feet from me at this instant, and it's time that she gets in it. Do not pass go! Do not collect a hundred dollars! Go to B-E-D.!"

She started whining, and this is what I heard from the back seat. "Mommy... Mommy... Mommy... Mooooommmmmyyyy... There's something in my heiney."

Now as a regular old run of the mill person, tell me, what can you say to that?

I was bumfuzzled. I asked her the usual questions. I was just running over just the high points because I was tired.

Me: Do you need to go potty?
B-Dubya: No.
Me: Have you already gone potty?
B-Dubya: No mommy. I'm dry. You can check.
Me: Did you stick anything in your pants? (Don't you dare judge! It's a valid question!)

B-Dubya: Nooooo Mommmy. There's something in my heiney.
It hurts mom.... *It huuuuurts!*

By the time I got out of the car, she was crying. When I pulled her out of the seat, she was dancing. I recognized instantly, it was too cold outside. I couldn't just strip her down in the great outdoors. I chose to send her into the house to the bathroom. In return, she chose to crab walk inside, sideways.

Halfway through the living room, she stopped and let out a yell. "IT'S BITING ME!"

By this time, I was completely anxious. I was at my wits end. Surely something was indeed attacking her! I mean I checked everything. She was dry. And she normally forgets even the important things within about two seconds. This was obviously a *big* problem! We went into the bathroom and I checked her pants for this intruder that was biting her.

And much to my shock, I realized... It was a wedgie.

She was only two. And yet, my daughter knew her colors. She knew her ABC's. She'd memorized the twenty-third Psalm. I honestly made the mistake of thinking she was some kind of a rocket scientist. But it became instantly apparent, she still had a LOT to learn.

~~~ ★ ~~~

Parenting Survival Tip # 12: Remind yourself often that you're doing the best you can. You're not a failure. It's not you. It's them.

B-Dubya and Captain A: (in unison) EWWWWWWW!!!

The Griz: What's Honey Badger doing that's gross?

B-Dubya: Licking a lion.

Me: (stepping in since further explanation was necessary) It's a sticky lion, slappy thing that sticks to the wall.

The Griz: (deep sigh and another inhale) Stop licking the lion son. It's been all over the walls and the floor. (then turning to me) He's disgusting. He's gonna catch herpa-gonna-syphal-itis.

Captain A: (contemplative, he's continuing the conversation in the back seat) I've tasted the floor.

B-Dubya: I ate a leaf once. And dandelions. But those aren't deadly. But we didn't know that at the time.

Dear God... Please make me a bird. So I can fly far... Far away. My brain just shut down. I. Can't. Even. Ever. Again.

~~~ ★ ~~~

Parenting Survival Tip # 17: You'll find yourself mediating the strangest arguments. Calm down. It's normal... Or that's what I tell myself to survive.

Captain A: (upon opening a present from his sister, he's *instantly* very offended) B-Dubya! Did you just buy me a girl dinosaur?

B-Dubya: (deflated and a little confused) Ummmmm... No.

Captain A: *THEN WHY IS SHE WEARING HIGH HEELS?*

Me: Seriously son? Relax. It's a T-Rex... His feet are just shaped that way. It isn't a conspiracy... Stop yelling.

~~~ ★ ~~~

Parenting Survival Tip # 18: Clarify! Clarify! Clarify!

Captain A: I'm hungry.
Me: That's good. What do you want for breakfast?
Captain A: A bloody egg.
Me: [blink blink]
Captain A: (breathless with excitement) You know mom! When
    you stab the egg... And its guts run out!!!!

Bloody eggs. Who knew? He's a boy. He's 100% boy... Even at
breakfast.

~~~ ★ ~~~

Parenting Survival Tip # 19: Even if you don't understand, their
fears are real to them.

I was greeted this morning by a grumpy little boy who came to
climb up beside me. His baby brother was still snoozing, and he
was bored. Instead of telling him to be quiet, I snuggled him for
a while and then asked him if he would be interested in going
out to the living room to watch something on Netflix until his
brother woke up. His response:

Captain A: I can't go out there. I'd be alone. And I'm afraid of
    the meerkats.
Me: Meerkats, son? Really?
Captain A: I'm not going out there. I had a bad dream about
    meerkats.
Me: Meerkats are nice baby. They eat grass.

Captain A: Not in my dream. They were vampire meerkats. They
bited people on the feet to turn them into other meerkats.

He stood true to his word. The child never left the room alone.

~~~ ★ ~~~

Parenting Survival Tip # 3: Don't ask questions. You really
*REALLY* don't want to know.

Me: Captain A, you're being obnoxious because you didn't get
enough sleep. Stop it. Or go back to bed.
Captain A: I'm only being og-noxious. . . (he takes a deep breath
with a long pause because he's thinking of a good excuse)
Because I have eyeball boogers.

*Really?!*

~~~ ★ ~~~

Parenting Survival Tip # 20: Always give precise instructions.

Honey Badger: (completely muffled) ARRRRRRRRGGGG
HHHH!
Me: (recognizing the cause of the muffled scream) Get off of your
brother's head.
Captain A: (in explanation) I'm not on his head. He's under the
blanket.
Me: (slightly concerned now) *Can he breathe?!?!?*
Captain A: Ummmmm... (he pauses and thinks hard, as though
this thought never occurred to him) I should probably check.

~~~ ★ ~~~

Parenting Survival Tip # 21: You *WILL* lose the conversation. Almost. Every. Time.

Me: I've seen a lion mixed with a tiger before. It was in a zoo.
B-Dubya: Wow! I've seen a zebra mixed with a donkey momma. It was weird.
Captain A: (refusing to be bested in anything...ever) That's nuthin. I've seen a chicken mixed with an alligator.

I've got nuthin' on that. You win the day son. You win the day.

~~~ ★ ~~~

Parenting Survival Tip # 22: You'll be faced with decisions you never dreamed!

Hypothetically... If a two-year-old purposely and with malice doth pull down the frog tank and crushes a tree frog named Killer Nightmare under a pile of florescent pink and purple rock rubble.

Hypothetically... If the mother of the little boy whose frog was unceremoniously murdered by the toddler doesn't take "Feed the Frogs" off of the daily chore chart.

Does that instigate ill-will towards the hypothetical two-year-old? Can the five-year-old even read yet? Will he notice/care if one of his chores aren't marked at the end of the day?

BLEH!!!

Decisions! Hypothetical decisions.

~~~ ★ ~~~

Parenting Survival Tip # 23: If you're going to laugh, you MUST do it silently... Annnnd out of eye sight.

I'm attempting to sing the ABC's with Honey Badger. He's happily joining in. Captain A begins singing. But he's singing in baby talk. No letters. Just confusion.

The Griz: Son, stop confusing your brother. If you want to sing the ABC's with him, that's good. Don't sing nonsense and made up stuff to your brother.

Captain A: I was singing in another language to him.

The Griz: Really son? (blink incredulous blink) What language was that?

Captain A: (without missing a beat) Korean.

The Griz: No. Son. Don't do it again.

Captain A: Actually... That was French.

I had to practice a *ridiculous* amount of self-control not to curl up under my desk laughing during this "teachable moment."

~~~ ★ ~~~

# Day 3

As I tucked my resentful daughter into bed last night, I smiled at the realization of where we've been. In the past twenty-four hours, she has had VERY little sleep and no nap and was somewhat grumpy. She absolutely doesn't get that from her mother.

But life now is more than where we've been in the last twenty-four hours. My mind plays over where we've been in the past three years. Approximately 1,381 days. Another measure of time is the 33,144 four hours since I found out I was carrying her. It seems like a long time. In that time, I've learned so much!

I've learned that sometimes, little girls just need to eat a hotdog for breakfast, with a banana no less. This, I've been told, balances things out.

I've learned that frogs are terrifying. Frogs are NOTHING to play with, not even the little plastic ones. Nightmares about these amphibians have plagued our home since she was big enough to speak.

I've learned that a cup of chocolate milk is enough to calm a calloused little heart, and return her to her pre-Hulk state of normalcy.

I've learned, that even though this sweet child can quote the entire twenty-third Psalm, she has *yet* to remember to not pick her nose in public (or during weddings... while walking down the aisle... as the flower girl.)

I've learned that long walks with mom and dad are desirable, not because she needs exercise, but because she knows that when she gets tired, she'll be carried. She'll be carried by one or both of us, regardless of how tired we are. She needs that security. It's comforting.

I've learned, that after walking a mile and a half, carrying a three-year-old is *murder*. She's heavy, and I'm tired.

I've learned, that mornings are a beautiful time to share with a fuzzy headed girl. And that little fuzzy haired girl wants to be in my bed, on my pillow, but won't tolerate morning breath. I've learned that there is a definite double standard. While her breath could melt steel, she's *quick* to point out the short comings of others.

I've learned that even though she loves school, she doesn't ever want mom to go to work.

I've learned, it's best to always keep the toilet bleached. A parent never knows when a stray bath toy, or an accidental little naked behind is going to plummet into the depths and need rescuing.

I've learned to hug her tightly and kiss her each night. Routines provide comfort. It helps her fall asleep.

I've learned, that orange flavored ibuprofen makes her barf, as does cantaloupe.

I've learned that she'll *insist* on going to the bathroom by herself. While it's hard to stand back, I've learned that standing back is necessary. And even though I *know* she still can't reach the light switch and *won't* go potty in the dark, I've learned that I have to wait until she calls me to turn on the light. She always realizes that she's not quite big enough, just like every single solitary time before. But I've learned that she needs to at least *feel* independent.

I've learned that it physically hurts me to see her hurting. With that comes the overwhelming realization that my mom wasn't joking when she said it hurt her worse to spank me than it hurt my behind.

I've learned that other kids can be mean spirited, and that I just need to listen when she tells me something. She's no angel. She can be a monster too, but she's a mostly honest monster.

Thanks to her, I've learned that raisins are hard to see on blue carpet and that chocolate doesn't come out of upholstery. I've learned that ketchup makes everything better, especially potatoes, and sometimes strawberries...

I've learned that my family is a gift from God. And I've learned that it's an undeserved gift, but cherished all the more.

I've learned not to take the moments for granted, because they pass too quickly. Nose picking and potty training disappear before you know it, and just that quickly, they're starting school.

Perhaps she'll have siblings one day and these moments will flash back. And if I'm lucky enough to have other children, in my sleep deprived state, I'll have to remind myself to cherish the little things.

I've learned to write it down. You'll soon forget the sound of a newborn's cry. The smell of a freshly lotioned little bathed behind, will be a fleeting memory. The feeling of being a superhero to someone who loves you unconditionally will melt into the frustration of the teenage years.

And as life goes on, I hope to never stop learning.

~~~ ★ ~~~

Parenting Survival Tip # 24: They will repeat it... Incorrectly. Ever. Single. Time. And it will be funny.

Me: Captain A, what did you learn about in Sunday school today?
Captain A: I drawed a horn.
Me: What kind of a horn?
Captain A: A horn of food.
Me: A horn of plenty? Why did you draw that?
Captain A: Because Aunt Dixie made me. And she had a glass one. That was breakable... Like a sheep.
Me: What was your lesson about?
Captain A: Baby Jesus. And the angel came to Joseph and said, "DON'T BE AFRAID OF THE DARK!" And then Mary was pregnant. And there was a baby in her tummy already. And he jumped and leaped for joy. And then he punched her. And that baby, he kicked her. And she was *very* mad. Because

she was so big. And he hurt her. And we will caaaaaall him Jesus. Cause he will save the people from their sins.

~~~ ★ ~~~

Parenting Survival Tip # 27: Yes. You just said that. Don't try to understand why.

The Griz: Son, put your hat and your egg down so you can go pee.

~~~ ★ ~~~

Parenting Survival Tip #3: Don't ask. You really *REALLY* don't want to know.

My morning situation.

Captain A is 'training' Wanda. You know Wanda. She's the dog who does nothing. NOTHING...Except eat. She does enjoy being loved. Captain A is currently losing. Wanda got a treat though, so she's happy.

Honey Badger is walking around announcing, "Good bye all people. Goooodbyyyyyeeee." I'm not certain as to why. I long ago learned not to ask questions.

And B-Dubya just informed me that she watched a horse give birth yesterday online, and she's traumatized.

Normal day… #carryon

~~~ ★ ~~~

Parenting Survival Tip # 28: Invest in solid door hardware.

There's nothing quite like the 'pleasure' of having a bout of morning sickness. Then there is the joy of morning sickness with a three-year-old spectator because you forgot to close the door fully.

I was told four times to "Stop that now."
I was asked about the brilliancy of the colors, not once, but *twice*.
I was asked if I was dying.
And I was given a handful of water... To make me, "Feel better *now!*"

Door locks are ESSENTIAL.

#LifeWithBoys

~~~ ★ ~~~

Parenting Survival Tip # 29: Sometimes, logic just doesn't work with kids.

Honey Badger is on one side of me, Captain A on the other. We're watching Shrek. Honey Badger wiggles and rolls across me, plopping down on his brother's side of my lap. Captain A is *truly* offended.

Captain A: *Get off my side!*
Me: Son, it's not that big of a deal. Just trade places. (patting the floor from whence Honey Badger came) Come over to this side.

Captain A: I caaaaan't Momma! There's a fart over there! Honey Badger left it. I heard it!

~~~ ★ ~~~

Parenting Survival Tip # 30: Sometimes, they won't need correction. Sometimes, they're right.

Captain A: I'm going to chop you! Haaaaaa! I chopped you!
B-Dubya: Oh no! Now I'm constipated!
Me: Decapitated. There's a big difference dear. It's decapitated.
B-Dubya: No mom. He chopped my rear end off. I'm constipated.
Me: Oh. My bad. Touche' dear. Correct usage. Carry on.

~~~ ★ ~~~

Parenting Survival Tip # 31: Don't *EVER* say yes before they finish the whole question.

Honey Badger: Momma... Can I look up your nose?

#ThatJustHappened
#HeHadAFlashlight
#BoysAreRidiculous
#WhatInTheWorld

~~~ ★ ~~~

# Day 4

A memory from August, 2010:

So today, B-Dubya came stomping into the house. It was *very* clear that she's flustered. When she gets flustered, her hair poofs more, and her freckles shine a little brighter.

It appeared, upon closer inspection, that she was mad at the dog. And her hair poofed, and her freckles shone. I mean, she was really upset.

I unknowingly asked her why.

"*BECAAAAAAAAAUUUUSE*"... she stated loudly and emphatically. "I told Allie to do a trick. And she didn't do it!" She was really miffed. I mean, she was disappointed with that dog for sure!

I asked her exactly what the dog did that was so bad. I just needed clarification.

"*Mooooom!*" She yelled, her frustration shining through. "I told Allie specifically that when I threw her food up in the air, that she was supposed to catch it." She paused for dramatic effect. "*Mom!* She just stared at me. And now there's a mess all over the porch. She's a bad dog mom. She never listens."

Oh yes she did.

The entire cup of food was strewn about the porch. What's worse? I have *zero* doubt she truly expected the dog to understand English and catch that food. Every single piece. And poor Allie had no idea why it was raining Kibble. Now the child is mad at her dog.

Some people just can't win. The logic of a five-year-old will absolutely blow the mind.

~~~ ★ ~~~

Parenting Survival Tip # 32: At some point, you'll be a surgeon, even if you don't plan ahead with eight years of medical school.

Honey Badger is mad at his father.

"Why?" Oh, I'm glad you asked!

The Griz just had to retrieve a Lego... From the three-year-old's flared right nostril. It was a one stud single block, gray.

He had to use tweezers. And it sounds like... The procedure hurt.

Apparently, dads make *horribly* unsympathetic surgeons.

~~~ ★ ~~~

Parenting Survival Tip # 33: Be honest. Be sincere. Be firm... Or the minions will lead you to insanity.

Captain A: (randomly musing) Daddy, how can a helicopter fly if it just has blades?

The Griz: When you're a little bit older, I'll be able to explain it. But if I try today, I'm just going to end up needing a drink.

~~~ ★ ~~~

Parenting Survival Tip # 34: Assume the worst. Then accept that it can go downhill from there.

An exasperated outburst from my husband in the hall bathroom with Honey Badger: Wash your hands! And put your underwear back on! What in the world is wrong with you?

I do believe the streaker... Is at it again.

~~~ ★ ~~~

Parenting Survival Tip # 37: Help them see the silver lining... Even when it's dim.

Captain A: (long and ridiculously drawn out) Uuuuuuuuuugggg gghhhhhhhh! I'm SO mad at you Honey Badger!

Me: Why are you mad at your brother?

Captain A: He ate my lipstick!

Me: Number one... It's chapstick.

Number two... He smells like Coke now.

Number three... He's moisturized and happy. You're a good big brother. Rejoice with him.

~~~ ★ ~~~

# Day 5

B-Dubya-isms. In our house, they're precious moments.

I'll share an example of her quick tongue. I heard my daughter singing in the car yesterday. She kept repeating the same thing over and over again.

"In the name of Jesus.... Get up and walk. Get up and walk. In the name of Jesus. Get up and walk. Get up and walk."

She proceeded to tell me about her Sunday school lesson. "Mom. There was a man, and Peter and John walked by."

She then breaks out in repetitive, off-key, oh so amazing lyrics again. "Peteeeeeer and John were waaaaalllllking by."

Now, I need to be extremely transparent. Though I love my daughter immensely, this song was dreadfully off pitch. Garage doors were flying up all over the neighborhood. My dental fillings dislodged and walked right out of my mouth. I mean, her pitch leaves *much* room for lessons. She continued, "And they saw a man lyin' there. And he stuck out his paw. And they saaaaiiiid. Silver and goooold have I none. But in the name of Jeeeeesusssss. Get up and walk. Get up and walk. In the naaaaame of Jesus. Get up and walk. Get up and wallllllllk."

Now, I'm going to give you a moment to digest what just happened. You might've missed it. In my house, I have to pay attention. Go back and re-read that last paragraph. Maybe you'll catch it.

I'm gonna have to have a talk with her teacher because my daughter was telling this story, and she changed lyin' man (aka one who is crippled and can't use his legs) Yeah... she changed "lying" man to "lion" man. Then she went so far as to add the fact that he stuck out his paw. Scroll back up. Read again. Oh yes she did.

I'm certain that wasn't in the song. But she said it twice. I'm absolutely certain that's exactly what she meant. So now, Peter and John not only have they healed a man by their amazing faith, but he was a lion man... Now *that's* a miracle!

It always makes me laugh to see how kids interpret things.

A little misguided... I should say!

That cracks me up until I really think about it. The Bible says that we must come to Him and have faith like a little child. My thought is that if I had the attention span of my daughter, and faith like my son, I wouldn't be able to find my way out of the bathroom each morning.

And then I think, how amazing would that be? No worries. No cares.

I tucked her in last night. On that particular night, she wanted to camp out on her floor. So I made a pallet, and gave her all of

33

her stuffed babies, climbed down beside her. On my way down to the floor I could only ponder how I would ever get up. Oh for the days when I was little and wanted to sleep in new places, experience adventure! I didn't have to worry about aches and pains or a sore back. I remember sleeping outside on my porch one night in a sleeping bag because I had begged my mom. We lived in the country, so who cared? I woke up soaking wet from morning dew and *freezing*. Why? Because I'm not the smartest cookie. I've never claimed to be the brightest crayon in the box. I *insisted* on sleeping outside. You get the picture.

So, I tucked my daughter in on the floor. All the while, I'm thinking, her apple doesn't fall far from my tree. We said our prayers. Mine are elaborate. I want to praise God and thank Him for the things He's done. I want to pray earnestly. I want Him to hear me. I want to repeat the same prayers I've said before, just in case He didn't get the memo the first time.

B-Dubya's prayer are simple. Last night they went like this:

"Thanks God. You love me. Thanks for my family. Help me not to have nightmares. Help me to sleep good. Help mommy to sleep in my bed please, if Daddy snores. Thank you God, for Captain A. And please be with my cousin. God, he has a crooked tooth. And we're not sure what we're going to do about that. But you can fix it. The end."

Yes. At the end of her prayers, she bypasses the traditional 'Amen.' She just says, "The end." But isn't that appropriate?

God. Thank you.

God. I love you.

God. I trust you.

The end.

I'm not going to pick this burden up and carry it.

The end.

I've prayed it and you heard me, and this is over. Now I'll sleep in your comfort, rest in your grace, and wake up tomorrow to do it again.

She didn't ask for bills to be paid, or health, or wealth.

She didn't think about tomorrow and its worries. She just thought about the right here, tonight. And she was done.

The end.

And it was a beautiful example of the fact that tomorrow can worry about itself. Tomorrow the sun will rise and set. Regardless of what happens, I still won't be in control.

Tomorrow I'll breathe and live and make a paycheck. I can either spend my time worrying, or relax and soak in the sunset. I can pray for rain and pack my umbrella knowing that He heard me the first time. I can believe in my God's amazing ability to heal and restore my broken places. I can trust Him.

Have faith like a child.

The Bible never says we have to have all the answers. The Bible never says we have to be right about all things.

The Bible doesn't mention a THING about a lame furry lion man sticking out his paw to Peter and John, but I bet my life that God heard that little girl's prayer.

I'd bet He listened too. And though I didn't end up sleeping in her room that night, and Rob's tooth is probably still crooked. I bet Adonai has amazing plans for faith like that.

~~~ ★ ~~~

Parenting Survival Tip # 38: Just nod, smile and keep moving. Recognize that they will indeed become productive members of society, even if it seems like a long stretch.

Honey Badger: Momma, I don't want my head to be a circle. Not anymore.
Me: What do you want it to be?
Honey Badger: Ummmmm.... A rep-tangle.

#logic

~~~ ★ ~~~

Parenting Survival Tip # 39: If you don't know... You just don't know. And that's okay.

B-Dubya: (looking at a loaf of dark bread) Mom, what's a pumpernickel?

Me: I have no idea. I asked your father. He didn't tell me. (He either didn't hear me, or he thought I was joking.)

Seriously... No clue.

~~~ ★ ~~~

Parenting Survival Tip # 40: Be glad it wasn't what you originally thought it was.

Have you ever...
Been walking to the kitchen at midnight...
Bare foot...
In the dark...
And felt a slight crunch and something squirt out from under the arch of your bare foot...
And had to muffle a silent scream...
Because you were *certain* you had just stepped on a massive pine roach that had crept in...
Or a mouse...
Only to slow your breathing... Shakily find the light switch... And sigh deeply to find...
You had stepped on...
A grape tomato?

~~~ ★ ~~~

Parenting Survival Tip # 43: Keep it clear and to the point. They do.

Me: Poor baby. Your nose is allllll stuffy.
Honey Badger: My nose sucks.

That was a clear and precise sentence from the two-year-old. The Russian linguistic judge gives that a ten.

~~~ ★ ~~~

Parenting Survival Tip # 44: Teach them the art of speaking quietly.

From the back porch, "Mom... Can ummmmmm... Can the dogs eat salt and vinegar chips?"

#1. Probably not the most nutritious.
#2. Wanda has prooooobably already stolen some.
#3. Don't speak so loudly. Those are your daddy's chips.

~~~ ★ ~~~

# Day 6

A memory from July, 2010.

I came home from work two days ago, and my happy daughter met me at the door. It was close to ten o'clock. I wondered what in the world was going on. Why was she still up? Not one to miss an opportunity at a rapt audience, she calmly told me about her day. I'll admit that I didn't hear some of it. I was tired. I zoned out. I try really hard to focus on her every thought while I'm home during the day, but I've been at work for eight hours. And by this time, she's normally in bed. Though it was a pleasant surprise to see her, my senses weren't prepared for the barrage of thoughts as I stepped in from work.

However, I do distinctly remember hearing, "Mommy we did this yada yada yada ... And I didn't take a nap... Yada yada yada... And guess what Mommy? When we were in the tub tonight, Captain A pooped in the water."

I set my belongings down and laughed out loud. It was a hearty chuckle, and I felt it all the way down in my toes. It wasn't funny that my son pooped in the tub. No. That's disgusting. But the funny part is that he did it while I wasn't home. These are the things that make a mother's heart swell with pride.

Way to go son! Way to finally give me a break!

I distinctly recall so many days when my husband came home to a battered woman when I was full-time, stay at-home mom. He constantly wore this "almost pity" look in his eyes. He didn't understand how desperate I was to see his face when he came home from work. I was always here, cooking meals and cleaning and lovin' on my babies. He knows I love those children, but he just didn't get it. He tried, but he just couldn't understand. Unless one has worn the hat of full-time-stay-at-home-parent, they just can't grasp the exhaustion. It's rewarding, but it's *hard*!

After this day, I think he got it.

I pulled myself together and came around the corner into the kitchen. I stopped laughing long enough to look for my other half. I found him. My husband was washing dishes quietly. He never broke stride, never looked up. Through the gentle suds and scent of Dawn dish detergent, he mumbled a quiet "Hello."

I walked over to him, smiling. He smiled back, but I recognized that smile. It wasn't a smile of "it's good to see you." It was the smile of the weary, the down trodden. Oh, how I knew that smile. I had worn it so many days before. All I could read on his face was, "This is almost over, and I get to go to bed."

I couldn't help myself. I burst out laughing again, and asked him how he was doing. I *could* have stayed silent. I *could* have pretended sympathy. But this was one of those golden opportunities that never come around. It was the equivalent of seeing a shooting star while watching the aurora borealis. It was like finding Jimmy

Hoffa's grave. It was a once in a lifetime moment. If I didn't ask the question, I may never have this moment again.

"Soooo... How was your day?"

He sighed deeply, and proceeded to tell me about his day.

He was tired when he got home from work. That's totally normal.

When he arrived, the kids were wired for sound and trying to think of new and inventive ways to solve the world hunger crisis. They apparently were doing all of this while playing the tambourines and burning down the house. He patiently prepared supper and fed them.

I took a moment to look down at the floor as my tired man was narrating his day.

There were noodles *everywhere*. It was very clear that ground zero was my son's high chair. I mean, it looked like a noodle factory blew up in my kitchen. They were spread in a beautiful pattern of chaos around and under the kitchen table.

The Griz pointed out that's only *part* of the mess. The other part he swept up. This. Is. Not. Cool. We're tryin' to be nice to the little guy, but discipline is definitely in order. He's messy by nature, but he's just recently become purposefully destructive. Honestly, that's not cute. I don't care who you are. That habit is going to have to die a quick death. Captain A will *not* be allowed to morph into a food thrower. The tossing of unwanted food onto my floor is a habit that *will* be broken. He's only one, so

I automatically win that round. I'm the parent, and he'll find it awfully hard to toss food in the floor with no arms. I'm just sayin'. Then, as an added bonus, he also wouldn't be able to pick his sister's nose or pull her hair, or dunk stuff in the potty.

*HEEEEYYYY!* That's actually not a bad thought!

I digress.

Back to the story, I refocus. The Griz finished making B-Dubya's supper juuuust in time to find Captain A's supper on the floor. I'm certain that wasn't a pretty scene. We don't go lightly on that stuff. We don't ignore it and smile and think he'll grow out of it. We tackle it head on.

By this part of the story it was clear that the hubs was exhausted. He made sure B-Dubya ate her supper, and then he inhaled his own meal. He needed to wind them down, so he ran a bath for the kiddos.

After he tossed the appropriate amounts of toys and children in the bathtub, he came out to grab towels and such. The kids never stay in there long, but they really do play well together. I mean, there's bubbles and noise! What's not to love?

According to the timeline of our eldest, the reporter, Daddy had only just stepped out of the bathroom when Captain A decided to poop in the water. She relayed with great vigor and flair, "It was gross Mom." Her narrative was concise, and dramatic. To hear her tell it, it was a smooth catastrophe averted. No strain, no stress, just handled gracefully.

Now to hear it from her father's perspective, that's not exactly how it went down. "I heard B-Dubya screaming," The Griz informed me. "I go into the bathroom and B-Dubya is attempting to climb the back wall of the tub, and Captain A's just sitting in the water with his floaters keeping him company. He was smiling at me. I would have been angry, but he was so happy. You can't be angry at that face." I stopped for a moment to imagine my son. He's always the giver. He's sooooooo happy to share a smile. He has confident assurance that he's the apple of his daddy's eye.

The Griz helped B-Dubya to disengage from her suction on the back wall and disembark from the water. He then looked at the tubby, happy child. I mean, what do you even do with that? There's a kid in the tub, and there's poo in the water. And I don't know about you, but I think there would be *no* more perfect moment to decide to go on vacation. Throw in the towel. You win! You and your sister can have the house. I'm out!

But The Griz is a better parent than me. As the next chapter in the story, he reached down and picked Captain A up, and then drained the water from the tub after pulling the toys out. Ewwww! I. Can't. Even.

He pulled the happy child out, hustled him back to our bathroom for a shower. In the process, he pointed B-Dubya in the direction of her pajamas.

Now, I want you to take a moment, savor, and imagine this: Captain A is fast. He's no joke when he's free and running loose. Though a shower is small, that's still a lot of space for a little tired kid to run circles while daddy is trying to hose him down with the extended shower head. The child was naked, slimy, soapy, and busily running laps.

In all seriousness, I would have left the house. My husband is a *trooper*! I mean, after his patience in handling this situation, he qualifies for a combat medal or something!

Finally, the shower was over, the kids in bed. Our nightly news reporter was evidently taking notes for her monologue to mommy later and the obligatory nightly report to CBS. Daddy then had to deal with the tub.

It grosses me out to even think about. The Griz holds no details back. I tried to block some of the story from my consciousness, but I do recall he used a trash bag. He relayed to me that the trash bag was rendered ineffective because everything in the tub was waterlogged and soggy. It was at that point in his story that I blacked out. I only felt my heart revive when I heard the word "bleach." All I know is that I missed a fairly large part of the story, but now my tub is clean.

Oh thank you Lord for my amazing hubby, who didn't give up and leave that soggy mess for me!!! Oh praise God for Captain A, who didn't wait until later to poop in the tub! He chose to share that sweet gift with his father, *before* momma came home in the midst of that fiasco.

I still laugh to myself as I think about the lengths to which my children will go to torture their father. You might think a seventeen-month-old doesn't comprehend the difference between right and wrong. I absolutely disagree. In fact, I would stake money that he and B-Dubya probably split a chocolate milk and an Oreo and planned this whole night out step by step. Captain A knew. I don't care what anyone says. That child knew. "Okay sis... On my signal, cue the screaming and climbing the walls. Daddy is tired. Let's send him to the psych ward. I'm working on my best poop face. Oooooh perfect! One... Two... Three... Goooooooo!"

The story ended without fanfare. I felt compassion welling up. I walked over and kissed my grizzly bear of a husband. He just looked completely defeated. I was still laughing to myself, but inwardly now, where he couldn't see. While preparing for bed he asked me if I was going to blog about this.

L...
O...
L...

Oh yes my dear. I most certainly will. I wouldn't bypass this golden opportunity for a whole bucket full of billion dollars bills.

My husband was weary. He was ready for bed. He was now thoroughly certain that the children were out to get him and that no one completely understands the depth of the pain of parenthood in our household.

He informed me that he didn't want me to misrepresent the situation. As he quietly walked towards bed, and I heard him say, "When you decide to write this story, PLEASE... Make me the victim..."

Oh how I love that man!

~~~ ★ ~~~

Parenting Survival Tip # 45: In the blink of an eye, you'll realize that your kids speak such wisdom sometimes!

Just finished reading book to Honey Badger called Peanut Butter and Jelly Brains.

It's about a little boy zombie who loves sandwiches, not brains.

Honey Badger hopped down from my lap.

I playfully moaned at him, "Braaaaainnnns, I'll eat your braaaaains!"

Matter-of-factly, he stated, "No, you won't. I don't have any brains. None of us kids do."

And with that, he marched down the hall.

I didn't even argue. In fact ... I quietly agreed.

~~~ ★ ~~~

Parenting Survival Tip # 3: Don't ask questions. You really *REALLY* don't want to know.

From the living room I just heard...

*STOP STANDING ON YOUR HEAD AND EAT YOUR LUNCH!*

That just happened.

~~~ ★ ~~~

Parenting Survival Tip #3: Don't ask questions. You really *REALLY* don't want to know.

We'd been swimming at a friend's house for a few hours. It was a birthday party. The kids had a blast. We returned home just before bedtime with a carload of worn out kiddos. Honey Badger was walking down the hall, and he stopped to ask me a question.

Honey Badger: Momma, do you remember at the party when I told you I needed to go potty?

Me: Yes. I remember. Why?

Honey Badger: (shrugs and quietly walks away)

Me: (realizing we were at a *pool* party, I needed to clarify his actions quickly) WHOOOAAA! Stop! Come back here! You said you needed to go potty, and now you don't need to go potty. Where did you go potty?

Honey Badger: Ummmm...

Me: No sir! You tell me. Where did you go potty, son?

Honey Badger: Ummmmm... In my shorts.

Me: Tell me you didn't pee in the pool.

Honey Badger: (sincerely) I didn't pee in the pool, Momma. I didn't!

Me: So, you peed in your shorts. (I needed answers. I don't know why, but I NEEDED to know.) Son, where were your shorts located when you peed?

Honey Badger: (matter-of-factly) It was just a little. My shorts were in my car seat.

47

Me: (horrified) *You peed in your car seat?*

Honey Badger: No. I peed in my shorts.

Me: YOUR SHORTS WERE IN YOUR CAR SEAT!

Honey Badger: Yes. But it was just a little bit.

Me: (trying to soothe my anxiety by minimizing the painful realization that I had failed as a parent) But you didn't pee in the pool?

Honey Badger: No! That's gross. Just in my shorts.

He walked on down the hallway to his bedroom, and I just accepted that. He didn't pee in the pool. At least he has *some* standards. I can work with that… Maybe.

~~~ ★ ~~~

Parenting Survival Tip # 46: They all have ants in their pantelones. And sometimes, they'll tell you about it.

I was trying to say, "Grab your spelling notebook. It's time to do spelling."

It came out, "It's time to do Spanish."

Without missing a beat, B- Dubya replied, "Hormigas…Hormigas en mis pantelones."

#SheDoesNotSpeakSpanish
#ILaughedOutLoud
#ThatKidIsQuick

~~~ ★ ~~~

Parenting Survival Tip # 47: Read between the lines!

Captain A: Momma... Can you get carpet burn from riding on
a skateboard... On your tummy... When the skateboard has
verrrrry spiky glitter on it?
Me: Son, just go put a shirt on.

~~~ ★ ~~~

Parenting Survival Tip # 48: Their friends are just as gross as
your own kids. Other parents might deny it… But kids are kids.

Me: Why are you all standing and staring at the pool?
Captain A: Because there's earthworms in the pool.
Me: *Why are there earthworms in the pool?*
Maddie: Well... I didn't want it to dry out.
Me: Now it will drown. Excellent.
B-Dubya: Earthworms don't drown. They swim.
Me: No. They drown.
Captain A: Ya'll are *so* disgusting! I'm not touching that thing.
It's big like a snake.
Maddie: Ummmmmm. Can I go in and sanitize my hands?
Because I touched that thing... And now I've been eating
cheese balls.

#facepalm

~~~ ★ ~~~

Parenting Survival Tip # 49: Sometimes when life is hard, you
can witness a glance of truth faith, deep faith. They're pure.

They're deep, even in the midst of the chaos. Listen to the heart of your children.

I'm sitting on the front step. I'm quiet. Life is very difficult at this point in our home. Finances upside down, and my husband is dealing with a life changing injury from his job. I'm needing time to sort my thoughts, and B-Dubya comes out to sit next to me.

B-Dubya: Whatcha doing momma?

Me: Just wondering how we can best glorify the Lord in this mess we're in... Life is messy right now. (tears are streaming, and I'm trying to capture my thoughts) How would you glorify the Lord baby girl?

B-Dubya: By having a stronger faith Momma.

Me: That sounds good. But what does that mean to you? How do you do that?

B-Dubya: Believing more... And still taking care of others... Even now. Don't stop.

[truth from a nine-year-old... attitude check]

~~~ ★ ~~~

Parenting Survival Tip # 50: Remember that in learning to read, evidently E's are EXTREMELY important to comprehension.

B-Dubya: (reading a book about dangerous creatures) *Mom!* Look at *this* wild beast!

Me: (before eight o'clock in the morning, and I'm trying to finish my coffee and open my eyes) Yes honey. That's amazing.

B-Dubya: He doesn't look scary. I wonder why he's in here.

Me: What is it?

B- Dubya: A wild beast.

Me: What kind?

B-Dubya: Just a wild beast mom. That's what it says. But he's not even scary.

Me: Hold up the picture again. (blink blink) Oh... Well dear, that's because it's a wildebeest.

~~~ ★ ~~~

Parenting Survival Tip # 51: Grow thick skin. Without it, you'll be offended... often.

Captain A: (singing with all his might) I'll do my best. I'll do myyyy best. Woooooahhhhhhh! I'll do my best for you.

Me: Wonderful! That means you'll finish your cereal without fussin'. I'm so proud!

Captain A: No Mom. It's a song. I was singing to God. Not you.

~~~ ★ ~~~

# Day 7

A memory from April 2010:

So, I'm hanging laundry on my porch tonight.

Why?

I'm hanging laundry because it's beautiful outside, and pollen isn't too bad. Plus, sun dried clothes are amazing. I enjoy the outdoors, the magic of my children's curiosity, the birds and flowers. Also, as an added bonus, technicality and side note, my stupid dryer is broken. Whatever... Lemons and lemonade, people. Lemons and lemonade.

I'm out on the porch hanging clothes, and I've let my children wander out into the great unknown that is our back yard. I look over the porch railing below, and I beam with pride.

My babies are sitting side by side in the grass.

B-Dubya has out her "special collection". All her most valued treasures are in her backpack, and she's been dragging that satchel around for hours. She's pretty particular when it comes to her things, but right now, she's sharing with her baby brother.

I watch quietly, taking in the moment, savoring the aroma of peace, amazed at God's goodness.

She hands little brother a rock. He works on his pacifier while thinking and carefully inspecting it. Captain A examines every single angle. This rock evidently passes the quality check.

"Need another one?" She pauses while he nods. "Okay."

This time she goes for the *really* special one, a treasure within a treasure! It's a sea shell. This is important! Captain A gently take it, studies it. He flips it over, staring at its workmanship. He grunts.

He then draws his chubby little arm *waaaaay* back and flings it into the grass. He tosses it as far as he can. Guess that seashell didn't pass inspection.

B-Dubya roars, "*NO SIR!* That's *MINE*. And it's special."

I hear a shocked little, "Sorry." Rather, it comes out, "Saw-wee." Add in a little teething two-year-old spit and a pacifier that causes a lisp... Yep. Perfect.

She scuttles out into the yard and picks up the shell.

The two of them continue just sitting there, passing rocks. They're enjoying the sunshine. They're happily soaking up the sun and smelling like sweaty little kids. If you have children, you know the smell. It's universal. It's the smell of summer. It's the smell of contentment and exhaustion, mingled with mischief and imagination. It's beautiful.

B-Dubya breaks the silence and pulls out her red squeezy water jug.

"Wanna drink Fat Boy?" He isn't offended. He knows that's a term of utter endearment. He's our little butterball, and we take delight in his rotundness.

"Yes." He states clearly, but it comes out, "Yeth." Add a touch of drool onto the last sound. Perfect! Now you've got it.

She holds it over her brother and gently squeezes the little jug into his mouth. There's a drool string as she pulls it away. I wait to see if she'll be insulted by the brother-spit. Instead, she merely grimaces, and wipes the bottle top on her shirt. She then takes a swig.

I watch quietly as they repeat the process several times. Tilting, drinking, swapping drool, wiping. Then on to sharing rocks, inspecting seashells. They both take another drink.

My heart is full. I'm liking this "Mom" thing at the moment. It's the little moments that mean so much.

Something in the atmosphere changes at that particular moment. B-Dubya pauses. I lean over a little further to see what is happening, but I don't interject myself into their moment. My daughter draws back with all her arm, she pulls back as far as she can possibly extend that fist. I note that she looks disturbed. Time slowed to a crawl, and I felt like my voice had disappeared into nothingness. I felt like I was running through Jell-O, or trying to fast walk in the shallow end of the pool. I couldn't get to my son, and it was suddenly *very* apparent that B-Dubya had a plan!

Captain A doesn't move. He's cautiously watching sister. His brow is furrowed.

She pulls back a touch further and then releases! Full throttle swing. She sucker punches him in his right arm.

Wham-O!!!

I freeze. The epic mothering moment was gone, dissipated into smoke and mirrors. I began preparing to come to the rescue of the toddler and to chastise the big one. I mean, she hit him hard!!! They were just innocently drinking water and then...

What in the world???

I glance over at Captain A. He's sitting, completely frozen. It's abundantly clear that he's NOT happy. He's glaring his sister down. His trusty paci is pulsing at a frenzied rate. He's got the "angry old man" furrow in his brow, and this momma knows it's about to get UGLY!

I take a deep breath.

B-Dubya then breaks the silence. "What?" she says so innocently. "It was an ant."

He just looks down at his arm.

Recognition hits, and I'm now laughing so hard I can't breathe. But I'm having to laugh quietly, lest I be spotted eavesdropping. I can't spank her. She just saved her brother's life. She was being the best big sister she could possibly be! It doesn't appear that Captain A is as merciful to her genuine act of devotion as she expected. He's *not happy* about being slugged. But B-Dubya is resolute, completely unapologetic. This was a necessary blow.

I come dashing inside to keep from hyperventilating. I got away with eavesdropping and not being caught!

What happened after that, I'm not certain. However, I'm pretty sure he forgave her. I'm pretty sure he didn't punch her back. He got over the shock of being walloped for no reason while he was rock admiring. He must have coped with the betrayal of being thwacked while innocently drinking water.

Now I'm a decent mother. I have strong, and a big heart. I'm honest about the fact that I'm flawed and imperfect.

But I don't care what you say...

That's funny.

~~~ ★ ~~~

Parenting Survival Tip # 52: Just smile and wave boys, smile and wave.

Me: Honey Badger, please go potty.
Honey Badger: I did. There's just none. There's no tinkle in my tinkler.

I have no idea how to even respond to that. Carry on.

~~~ ★ ~~~

Parenting Survival Tip # 53: If you listen carefully, you'll hear the sound of a million song writers being offended at the misquoted lyrics.

Captain A: (at the top of his little lungs in the back seat of the car) HE BROKE THE FRECKLES OFF MY FEET SO I CAN DAAAAANCE!!!

Me: Ummm... Son, if we're singing about Jesus... I'm pretty sure the word is 'shackles'... Not freckles. But that's just a suggestion.

~~~ ★ ~~~

Parenting Survival Tip # 3: Don't ask questions. You really *REALLY* don't want to know.

Captain A: (excitedly) *Mom!* My new gloves didn't get ruined when I washed them!

Me: (blink ... blink) Son... Did you just wash your new gardening gloves in the bathroom?

Captain A: YES! And they aren't ruined mom!

Me: (on a parenting hunch) Son, by chance, did you just go potty while wearing your new gloves?

Captain A: Ummm... (with a hint of "don't be dumb" in his intonation) Yeah mom... That's why I had to wash my gloves.

~~~ ★ ~~~

Parenting Survival Tip # 52: Just smile and wave boys, smile and wave.

Captain A: Momma, have you ever seen a caterpillar turned into a butterfly?

Me: When we were little, I remember finding cocoons and putting them into jars and waiting for them to change.

Captain A: So, you kept pet butterflies?

Me: No. When they changed, we let them go.

Captain A: Why?

Me: (wanting to give him an easy life lesson) Son, do you know what butterflies eat?

Honey Badger: I do!!!! I do!!! Butterfly food and possums.

~~~ ★ ~~~

Parenting Survival Tip # 54: Know for certain that words have double, triple, quadruple meanings.

Honey Badger climbed up on my bed and turned on the television. I wasn't paying attention.

He then asked, "Momma. Who is that chocolate guy?"

I must admit, I turned my head expecting to see a man of the same complexion as my husband.

Nope, there was no dark-skinned chocolate man on the screen. Instead, I was looking at a very pale Johnny Depp.

"That's Willy Wonka son."

Carry on.

~~~ ★ ~~~

Parenting Survival Tip # 3: Don't ask questions. You really REALLY don't want to know.

Captain A: I can't find my light stick. *Mom!* Don't drive! *I can't find my blue glow stick!*
Me: Calm down. I'm stopped. Unbuckle and search for it. It glows son. It's dark in here. You can find it.
Captain A: (frantic now... standing up in his car seat... ready to cry) I can't find it momma. It's *gooonnnee!*
Me: Son, I think your pants are glowing. Your backside... It's glowing blue. Why is it even in your...No. Don't tell me. Never mind. I don't want to know.

~~~ ★ ~~~

Parenting Survival Tip # 52: Just smile and wave boys, smile and wave.

Captain A: Look Maddie. Look. Venom is a bad guy. Look at him! He's got *reeeeaaally* hairy armpits.
Maddie: I know. That's what makes him a bad guy. Bad guys are sooooo disgusting.

~~~ ★ ~~~

Parenting Survival Tip #55: They'll work out their differences. Most times they can even do it without bloodshed.

Maddie: Whatever.... Spiderman isn't even real.

Captain A: (Incredulous) Uggghhhhh... Yes. Yes, he is.

Maddie: No. No. He's not. Spiderman is fake.

Captain A: You don't even know what you're talking about.

Maddie: Well... What about all the people who get their houses broken into in our subdivision? He doesn't even save them. People steal their stuff.

Captain A: (rolling his eyes and speaking slowly so that she understands how flimsy her argument is) WE. DON'T. LIVE. IN. NEW. YORK. CITY. That's why bad guys can steal our stuff.

[check... and mate]

~~~ ★ ~~~

# Day 8

A memory from March, 2011:

It should bother me that my husband and I recently had a minor disagreement about the evils of throwing away Tupperware. It's indeed a valuable commodity in our home. However, this doesn't fluster me. I'm not bothered. I'm not upset.

Tupperware is good. I'm in agreement with that. I have no qualms with that statement. Tupperware reduces waste. Tupperware is the holder of all that's tasty and re-heatable and salvageable with dinner. Tupperware is a life saver on the night after when I'm exhausted, and I realize there are leftovers. Tupperware saves time.

"Tupperware is good," said my husband. And deep down inside, I knew he was right. I mean, I so agreed on so many levels. I contemplated giving in...

No. Not this time. No. Reality set in. Then I shook my head and went for the kill shot in this conversation. Not just no... I placed the container in the trash two days ago. I was not losing this battle. Not this time. Not on your life. There was a time and a place for compromise. This. Was. Not. It.

Marriage is an incredibly complicated and beautiful series of compromises. Marriage consists of laughter and tears. Marriage is, "you can have a few hours with the guys at the gun show... if I can run to the mall by myself tonight."

Marriage is "I'll cook dinner... if you'll do the dishes."

Or...

"I'll bathe Things #1 and #2, if you'll put them in their pajamas. I'll feed the dog while you brush the kids' teeth."

Overall, marriage is wonderful. The Griz and I don't normally argue. We really do get along well. We're learning the art of compromise. Now, no mistakes, we're certainly not perfect. We just recognize that we have been forgiven. In turn, we're willing and able to forgive.

But on this particular night, I absolutely was NOT losing this battle. No matter how many deep sighs I heard about the evils of sacrificing Tupperware, I was not caving in. I. Was. Not.

The thing is, I understand that he didn't want me to throw this away. I mean, he wasn't being unreasonable. For the love of sweet Betsy, *it's Tupperware*! Tupperware is priceless!

But...

This particular Tupperware...

Had turkey in it...

Wait for it.... Wait for it...

This Tupperware contained turkey...

From Christmas...

Just mosey on up and take a look at the date on this memory. Let me help you...

It was written... In March.

Again... Tupperware. Turkey. Christmas. March.

So, I was being lectured about not throwing away Tupperware, but I NEEDED to win this battle. My very life and existence depended on not losing this issue. But we do compromise in our home, so I said sweetly, innocently, "That's fine. We can keep the Tupperware...If you clean it out." End quote.

Now, keep in mind that in marriage, it's not normally a good idea to gloat in the midst of one's triumphs. I normally follow that rule.

But on this day... I'm loud and proudly stating...

The Tupperware was picked up by our garbage men at 9:53AM. It's gone forever. And I'm washing my hands of the incident.

God bless the men and women who work our trash route.

Oh, one more thing!

P.S. to my Mother: You know that clear Tupperware container that was about two inches deep and rectangular? It had a white lid. It has been missing from your house since Christmas.

Yeah. Ummmmm, I'll replace that.

~~~ ★ ~~~

Parenting Survival Tip # 56: Just laugh, and let 'em sing.

Honey Badger: (singing at the top of his lungs) Wish we could turn back time, to the good ol' daaaaaaaaaaaaaaays, when our momma sang us to sleep, but now we're stressed out.

Please note: This lil' fella still wears pull-ups to bed, and takes a nap with his momma. Every. Single. Day.

I note the irony.

~~~ ★ ~~~

Parenting Survival Tip # 57: Praise the Lord when you realize your partner is as epic at this parenting thing as you are.

Captain A: Daddy, why does your body have blood?

(pause... crickets chirping while trying to figure out how to explain the circulatory system to a four-year-old)

The Griz: Ummmmmmm... It's kind of like juice son. It keeps your body from drying out.

~~~ ★ ~~~

Parenting Survival Tip # 12: Remind yourself often that you're doing the best you can. You're not a failure. It's not you. It's them.

Dear husband,

Your brand-new Bible... You know the beautiful one that our pastor gave you? It *might*... Ummm... Hypothetically... Possibly... Have teeth marks in it. But no worries! He only got the table of contents. I caught him before he ate the book of Genesis.

#ATeethingLearningExperience

~~~ ★ ~~~

Parenting Survival Tip # 58: Sometimes you need to step in to deescalate before there is sibling bloodshed.

Captain A: (adamantly... loudly... with force) *Honey Badger...*
    *Don't get on my bed.*
Honey Badger: (muted giggles) Yes. I will.
Captain A: (totally distraught) GET OFF OF MY BED! YOU'RE
    NAKED! GET OFF MY BED!
Honey Badger: Uuuuuuhhhhh nope.

~~~ ★ ~~~

Parenting Survival Tip # 3: Don't ask questions. You really *REALLY* don't want to know.

Honey Badger: Momma do you know what a nookie is? Well... It's your behind. I have one and if I show it, it will explode. And if you go to the beach, the sharks will bite it off. And well... That would be sad.

[What in the world just happened here?]

~~~ ★ ~~~

Parenting Survival Tip # 59: Your bark must be big and ferocious, so that you rarely have to use your bite.

On the front lawn, the boys are playing football. My hubs just walked outside to grab the mail.

I just overheard, "If you hit my car... I'll kill you. I need you to understand that."

And two mumbled, "Yes sirs."

Child rearing... At its best.

~~~ ★ ~~~

Parenting Survival Tip # 60: Run! It's an emergency this time.

From the bedroom down the hall...

Captain A: *Awesome*! B-Dubya! Your frog is playing dead!

[This doesn't bode well.]

~~~ ★ ~~~

Parenting Survival Tip # 61: If there's a bad word, they'll *always* hear it.

Captain A: Whoa turn that off! It's *soooo* inappropriate!!!! What he said... Unacceptable.

Me: Seriously... That kid is speaking in Spanish son.

Captain A: Well.... (blink blink blink) it *sounded* inappropriate.

~~~ ★ ~~~

# Day 9

A memory from February, 2011:

Tonight I put on my "teacher" hat. This isn't new. Teaching comes along with the role of "parent" and "mother." Teaching is a necessary part of those little ones growing up and getting their own wings. So I always try to teach.

Sometimes, I guide soothingly.

Other times, I shamelessly rant.

Who is throwing stones here? I'm human. Never claimed to be an angel. Nope, I'm a mom.

So, this night... We brought out the word cards. I had printed them the night before. They have the most basic sounds that we use to configure words. It's elementary, but if B-Dubya can recognize the core handful of basic group sounds, then it's a successful day.

We'll work on ridiculous English words like "necessary" and "restaurant" later. Not even kidding, I *never* physically hand write those words. And when I spell them on a computer, even now as an adult, I always wait for the squiggled red lines underneath. They *always* appear. I *always* right click, then choose the correct spelling from the list of possible suggestions. Every. Single. Time.

I digress.

So we were doing word cards tonight. I was rocking it out, trying to make it fun. Captain A was napping peacefully. It was just me and B-Dubya.

Daddy was in the next room on his computer, randomly shooting glances and questioning my sanity.

"O-U-S-E," I spelled out the letters. It's pronounced, "ooowwwwsssee". Nice and slow going was this teaching lesson. "Ouse' is the sound that happens when the letters O-U-S-E sits together." She's still small, so I was just trying to break it way down and force things to make sense.

I continued on, "Sometimes letters pair up. When they sit next to each other, they're like happy as a couple. Letters are a happy couple, like me and dad. Except your dad and I don't just sit together and make noises."

From the other room, I heard a low voice, "Sometimes I do."

I thought to myself that he'd better zip it. Flatulence and burps don't count in my teaching lessons.

On we go! No time to stop. "O-U-S-E B-Dubya. What word uses that sound?"

"House!" She shouts. "Mom! I did it."

Boy, was I proud! But I had to gently remind her about the sleeping Thing #2. No more shouting. It was certainly good to see her excited about reading though. We went on to spell "mouse" but not "louse." They give me the heebie-jeebies. We avoid words that cause physical reactions in our home.

"W-H," I say. "W-H makes a sound like a whistle... or whipped cream."

"Cool mom. Whhhhhh... I got it." She was acing it! I mean, she was just blowing through the hurdles.

On to the next sound!

"I-T-C-H." I showed her the card, so that she could sear the sound into her memory. "Like when you scratch your arm. I-T-C-H spells itch." I didn't think it wise to play around with this set of letters. I just stopped while I was still above water on this one. "Itch, stands alone." End of story. When a person plays with fire, sometimes there is smoke. Sometimes however, a full-fledged volcano opens up and devours everything in its path. My daughter is the volcano type. I wasn't giving her that opportunity.

Rolling. Steady. More letters. More sounds. We were on the move I tell you!

"E-E," I said, and up came the card for her memory. "E-E sounds like the little piggy who cried all the way home. When two e's stand together, they're loud and proud. E-E says eeeeeeeeee."

"Eeeeeee," she repeated rather loudly, which prompted a look from Daddy-Dearest, keeper of the volume controls in our home.

Never mind that. On we went, whizzing through more sounds. "O-W, says Ow... Like how and wow."

She placed a 'B' in front of the 'O-W.' I paused for a moment, considering the fact that there were multiple ways in which to pronounce this word.

A random flash of panic went through my brain. It was the first time I considered that I had started a task I couldn't even dream of winning. The voice screamed out to me, "You're not adequate for this. English is a stupid language. It would be easier to teach the child to read Arabic or Polish. She's never going to get a job if you're her only means of learning to read." On and on the voice went, until I had nearly convinced myself that this child was going to be living with me for the rest of my known existence, and she'd never be able to cook or read a recipe.

Still we pressed on.

The next letters we steamrolled over were, 'O-N' and 'O-R.' She carefully placed an 'R' in front of 'O-R' and sounded out, "Roar." I admit it. I didn't correct the spelling at that particular moment. I only praised her eagerness.

I kept thinking, "Just get her started. This is a good thing. Stupid words can be tackled later."

It was at that moment that we had a hard letter combo to deal with.

"I-G-H-T," I sounded out. "That's a tough one, but those letters together are very important. Here's an example baby girl. How many times do I have to tell you? Turn off the _____." I waited with baited breath. I was hoping she'd fill in that blank.

Boy did she fill it in with vigor! She hollered, "*Light Momma!* The light! I-G-H-T spells light!

"Yes." I said quietly. "Now hush it, or daddy's gonna make us both go to bed for being too loud."

I kept trying to think of inventive words for 'I-G-H-T.'

Found one! "The sun hurts my eyes. It's very _____." Again, I wait patiently.

She didn't disappoint. She had an answer ready. "Shiny mom. The sun is shiny. And you need to get glasses."

"Bright, dearest daughter of mine. The word is bright. See? I-G-H-T. The sun is bright."

A little downtrodden voice responded, "Oh... right mom."

I didn't want to end this sound on a bad note, so I thought up another example in my head.

Looking back on this night, I can admit now that I took a risk with words. It was a risk I shouldn't have taken. I'm owning my mistakes. I dove into the deep end without a life preserver. I said,

"This one is a good word. Think hard about I-G-H-T. Mommy is sitting down, and her pants are very _____."

"Fat."

One word. She responded with one, three letter word. She responded with one word and stated it like it was fact.

Teaching moment or not, I immediately wanted to throttle her. I wanted to give up. I quickly glanced into the other room, but not a single sound was muttered. I *know* that man heard the conversation, but suddenly, he was all caught up in his online activity. I think he's a *very* smart man.

I tried to redeem myself with dignity, pretending this painful moment was rolling off of me, like water off a duck's back. "The word is tight, not fat. I-G-H-T. Tight." I wanted to be gracious, so I reluctantly added, "But good try."

It was at that moment, that the child had the nerve to attempt to correct me. She, matter-of-factly stated, "Momma, tight and fat mean the same thing." She had no idea how very close to death she was. So verrrry close. And she didn't even know it. Bedtime. It needed to be bedtime. Bedtime would be her safest bet.

"Yes honey," I breathed deeply. I inhaled enough oxygen to make my brain spin. My nostrils just sucked up all the air around me. I needed it to clear out the visions of what was about to happen if she kept speaking. "But fat isn't what we're discussing."

My mind wandered for a moment. Some animals eat their young at birth. I should have taken that up as a hobby.

Back on course. I needed to get back on course. "We're talking about I-G-H-T. And we're talking about words that rhyme."

"Oh mom. Okay." Back on task. She was so simplistically innocent. She meant no harm.

For the good of all people, my blood pressure, and my daughter's health, I changed the subject.

We went on to review. I thought it would be good to go over a quick recap of all we'd accomplished tonight. I flipped through the word cards. Surprisingly, we'd actually done quite a lot. We'd switched letters, dropped consonants, and sounded out vowel combos.

The child decided that she wanted a piece of cake. I didn't have a problem with that but I needed to flip through the list one more time. A quick run through was all I wanted, just to solidify this lesson in her head. We hurried through. We made words up. We sounded them out. We pieced them together. We accomplished it. She survived.

We were almost finished. We were so close. Then we came across the 'I-G-H-T' card again. I took a deeeeeeep breath.

She smiled and looked into my eyes. She then put a 'T' in front of it. After that, the child smiled at me.

This kid had no clue how close she was treading to being mauled. Deep inhalations were in order again. In and out. Innnn and ooouuut.

"Mommy..." she whispered. "I did it. I can read. T-I-G-H-T." She spelled. "Tight... for your fat pants. Look dad! I spelled tight!"

He actually smiled at her. The look on his face indicated that he didn't think this would be a justified throttling. I stared at him. He was proud of her. I thought to myself that I had married a traitor, a dirty rotten no good traitor.

I wasn't sure about her, but I was *done, finished, through.* We cleaned up. I deep sighed and gave her a kiss. I told her I was proud of her. I prepped her for bed. I washed dishes.

And I vowed from that moment forward that I wouldn't be teaching her to read English.

Chinese. Chinese would be a better bet. There is no 'I-G-H-T' in that language.

~~~ ★ ~~~

Parenting Survival Tip #62: Perhaps we shouldn't assume so much from one sentence or phrase we hear or see.

Perhaps giving the benefit of the doubt isn't such a silly thing when we don't know people's motivation. Conversations with little people can be really... really good.

Honey Badger just burst into my room. He had bright eyes and a bushy tail. He vaulted up on the bed and sat down beside me.

Me: What are we going to talk about?
Honey Badger: Fat people.

[Pause for a moment. This is uncomfortable territory, mostly because I've struggled with my weight and appearance as long as I can remember. But we don't skirt away from truth in this house. We don't sugar coat, but we also don't encourage abusive conversation. So, I followed this trail to see where it would go. With a three-year-old... And I got schooled. He's honest, but his heart is genuine. I was the one who was uncomfortable. I should've known he wasn't being malicious.]

Me: Honey Badger! You just... You can't do that.
Honey Badger: But one day, we were at the grocery store... And there was a fat person.
Me: (trying desperately to change the subject) Honey Badger. Let's talk about dragons.
Honey Badger: (adamantly) No. Fat people. Because I like them. They're my kinda people. They're my favorite.
Me: We *are* good to hug.
Honey Badger: Yup. I already know. That's why I like 'em.

And that was that. Conversation over. He climbed down off the bed and ran off to play.

Parenting Survival Tip # 63: Sometimes you'll regret asking questions out loud. Ask anyway.

As I was getting ready for service this morning I had this nonchalant conversation...

Me: It sure would be nice if I knew where my black tights were.
Captain A: The last time I wore them, I took them off and put
    them on your bed.

#LifeOfASuperHeroMom
#GuessOneSizeDOESFitAll
#LifeWithBoys

~~~ ★ ~~~

Parenting Survival Tip # 64: Just appreciate the good. MOST days, the good moments far, far outweigh the bad.

That moment... When you're marveling at how incredibly sweet your youngest is when he's sleeping on you. You silently thank God for these precious moments you're lucky enough to have daily with these babies.

And as you're thanking the Father for His blessings... Your hip gets hot... And there's the sensation of wetness.

~~~ ★ ~~~

Parenting Survival Tip # 65: Always, ALWAYS keep extra teeth on hand.

I just walked down the hall. I wasn't even trying to check on the kids. As I passed by the boys' bedroom I hear, "Don't worry mom. I was just looking for dentures."

~~~ ★ ~~~

Parenting Survival Tip # 66: They'll get it right… Eventually.

Mow-lawner: [noun] a machine used for cutting grass according to the five-year-old.

~~~ ★ ~~~

Parenting Survival Tip # 30: Sometimes, they won't need correction. Sometimes, they're right.

Captain A: Mommy, I need new pants. I think I wet my bed.
Me: (groggy and still asleep) Honey, you couldn't have wet the
    bed. I put you on the potty already.
Captain A: Well… I…. Ummmm… Maybe I was drooling then…
    And maybe it got on my pants…

#ThatsLogical
#WakeUpAndHelpTheLittleFella
#BlessHisHeart

~~~ ★ ~~~

Parenting Survival Tip # 67: Be careful when you're packing for long road trips.

Captain A: (indignantly) *Moooom!* You can't pack that together! My Spiderman costume is *not* a toy Momma! It's not!

Me: (prodding the bear) Oh no! What are you ever going to do if a bad guy comes?

Captain A: (completely serious and looking at me like I'm the ridiculous woman who has doomed our house to certain death should a bad guy come) I don't know. You packed my suit. Now I can't save the world.

~~~ ★ ~~~

Parenting Survival Tip # 53: If you listen carefully, you'll hear the sound of a million song writers being offended at the misquoted lyrics.

Captain A: (singing loudly from the back seat) Feet life... Feet life... Whoa-oh-oh-oh-ooooooooh!!!

Me: The song says "*Speak* life. *Speak* life." Get it together son. Get. It. Together.

~~~ ★ ~~~

# Day 10

A memory from January 2011:

The next time I have a hair brained idea, I'm hoping my husband will give me 'the look.'

You know the look that says. "Alright. I give up. Be dumb. I'll still love you anyway."

He gave me that look Saturday. But on Saturday, I didn't heed it. I was too engrossed in being a home owner. I was too excited with the fact that I can drill holes in my own walls... Without asking permission.

I mean, honestly, that's *exciting*! Just ask me.

When I lived at home, my Mom and Dad let me mural my walls... But I had to ask.

When I've lived in some places, they were rented, and I could only hang pictures... NO PAINT!

When I moved here, I signed my life away until at *least* 2030.

And it's mine.

Well, to give proper credit, this house is a gift from God. He allowed me to sign the title, and I'm so thankful to have a solid place to call my own.

So since it's our home, I don't have to ask if I want to install surround sound and wire it through my own attic.

Now, if you're a home burglar who scans through books looking for the next house to break into, please save your breath, your time, and your crowbar. This sound system is *nowhere* near top of the line. We just purchased a house. Now, I can hardly afford to buy toilet paper. I saved for this for my hubs for his Christmas present, mainly because I couldn't afford to get what he really wanted. But to him, all electronics are good electronics. And no worries because he loves me anyway.

So I bought him a surround sound system, all 5 speakers worth. And I've been staring at them for over a month, sitting on top of our entertainment center... Since Christmas. I'm fairly certain they're mocking me.

And this Saturday was the day.

Oh was it ever!

This day, we were going to hang the speakers! "We can hang them neatly with clips to hold the wires." says hubby.

I told my husband I didn't want wires hanging here and there. I wanted it to be hung neatly.

He mentioned that could be accomplished only through the attic.

"No worries." I thought.

"Piece of cake." I thought.

Saturday I began to set up the day. I set up rather impatiently, I'll admit. My husband didn't balk. He gave me the aforementioned 'look,' but he didn't fight me. I've realized that sometimes his refusal to fight me just allows me to be dumb. And in these moments, he's kind enough that he doesn't say a word. He knows eventually I'll either kill myself, or learn a lesson.

To date, I've learned a LOT of lessons... But only after almost killing myself.

On to the attic! We can do this! Yes we can!

Kids were up and running around. They were desperately hoping to catch a glimpse up the attic stairs. It's the highlight of their somewhat sheltered lives. I offer no apologies. It's the simple things that keep us going. Let them peek up into the strange abyss, then go on about our days.

I was so excited! Up I went, broom in hand. I was cleaning as I went, sweeping insulation, pink dust bunnies flying.

I want you to get a firm mental picture.

On this day, I was wearing sweatpants. They're a Saturday fave. I was also wearing my husband's sweatshirt which happens to be 'slightly' larger than my size. It's a 4XL. I'm just an XL. I was wearing a headband hat thing that had a light attached to the front. So I honestly looked like a coal miner who was wearing someone else's clothes and didn't own a mirror. Top that look off by adding the most attractive feature. On my face, rested a dusk mask, held firmly in place by attaching to a messy bun on the back of my head. I was *good to go*.

I was the epitome of sexy housewife in action! Especially on that day, I had that part *doooown*.

Oh yes, I shouldn't fail to mention that there was also a snot stain on my left shoulder from my toddler. I was rockin' beat up tennis shoes and off to the attic I went with broom in hand.

Nothing could dampen my spirits. Life was good.

I stepped over boards. I swept as I went. I found studs. No. No. Not manly men, but rather solid boards on which to firmly plant my feet in the attic. If there *were* men up in our attic, either my husband or I would burn the place down. There's just no room for freeloaders in our storage space.

So there I was, sweeping, sweating, and finding places to step. I was thinking I was good at this.

When I began this story, I casually forgot to mention that I've always struggled with claustrophobia. It's been an intense struggle for most of my life. Claustrophobia plays an important role a little later in this tale. An intense fear of confined spaces can damage a person. I mean, I can't even sleep with my sheets tucked in around my feet. Never mind that silly detail though, I was on fire!

I swept my way down the main support beam of the attic, finding stepping boards like a professional. I was working my outfit too. Feelin' fine! Dust bunnies were congregating and dissipating as I made my way through the darkness with my coal miner's headband.

I looked slightly to the left and see the corner where the wires were supposed to go.

*Gulp...*

The area I needed to get to was on the other side of the fireplace. It's notable to point out that our fireplace sits under a vaulted ceiling. This corner of the living room has a place where the roof extends downward. It's there that the roof and the vault pitch together, trailing downward, into a tiny little corner. That tiny little corner, is directly above my entertainment center. That tiny little small, itty, bitty corner, well... That was the final destination. It's also now known in our home as ground zero, my nemesis.

I had a choice to make at that moment. I could continue, or I could back out. And I was not about to give in. I had made my stand. I did *not* want wires strewn through my living room. I *would* conquer my fear. I wouldn't back down and look silly in front of my husband. I wouldn't be defeated. And I wasn't about to admit that I was wrong. To admit failure would go against my very DNA.

Keep it moving! That was my motto that day. *KEEP IT MOVING!*

I did.

I climbed back up in the attic about seventy-three and a half times. I shooed Captain A away from the ladder so many times as to make myself hoarse. I finally gave in and allowed B-Dubya to go up and peek.

And now the moment of truth had arrived.

I went up again… The last stand. The final hurrah.

The Griz was drilling holes. Working together, and giving directions from either side of the drywall, we finally made ends meet and got two speakers hung. We ended up using our cell phones like walkie-talkies since all I could hear was my children through the attic opening. The heat was making it hard to focus. They were loud, and they don't know a thing about home hardware installation.

The Griz was on the phone with me. We got the first wire through without any trouble. It was then that I noticed that my leg had begun to slightly cramp from squatting. "No worries," I thought. This will be over soon. Two more holes to go.

Hole number two was in the corner of the room opposite side. It was a little more difficult to get to. It required a little more flexibility, and a prayer or three. There was another cramp. I worked through it. I didn't mention it to The Griz. He would have tried to give me silly advice on "not dying" up there, and who needs that kind of negativity?!

I wasn't going down for water. That would have taken too long. So what I had only had coffee to drink so far. So what! Only one hole to go. The last wire, in the far corner.

I began the ascent over the fireplace.

Now I know that I mentioned claustrophobia. Please understand that's not the only phobia I'm plagued with. I also have "height-a-phobia" or as I call it, "scared of falling through the ceiling while wearing sweatpants and killing myself in my own living room while wearing a dust mask and a head lamp, looking like a mole from a Disney movie a-phobia."

I didn't wanna die like that. There's no dignity in a death like that. There's nothing left for the obits. I'd go viral, for all the wrong reasons.

So, I began the ascent, and I noticed that my breathing had changed slightly. But I'm nothing, if not stubborn. I wasn't wavering! My husband wasn't going to be able to be "right". I was completing this task, even if it killed me.

Famous last words.

Up I went. The Griz was chatting with me on the phone. He was making small talk. I, at that moment however, wasn't feeling very chatty.

I reached the precipice and looked down into that little bitty tiny corner that I was destined for. It was the final stop on a so far successful journey. It was my Atlantis.

It was... tiny.

I looked down at the size of my hips, and again at that corner. Hips... Corner. I imagined a moose trying to hula hoop. Funny perhaps... But not very practical for the moose. Moose should find better ways of self-entertainment.

I immediately started fasting and praying.

This wasn't going to be good. Red lights were flashing in my head as gulped in a bit of air, and began the slope downwards.

It was hot. I mean, it was really, *really* hot. And I noticed to my dismay that the attic around me seemed to be spinning. It was only a slight spin, not enough to make me abort the mission. But warning sirens were screaming too... Mostly just in my head.

My hubby was still chatting with me. I didn't mention the spinning room or the sirens. I was taking it one step at a time, one joist, one step, one breath, one inch closer to the end of the mission.

I was going down, and the room was disappearing. I realized to my dismay that I was balancing exactly over the center of the tippy top of the family room fireplace.

I heard my children through the phone, down there safely on the ground. They were playing. I began to wonder what their next mother would look like. I prayed that she would at least be homely, so that The Griz would still be able to appreciate the woman I was. If he replaced me with a practical woman who was also beautiful? I'd be forced to haunt him for the rest of his life.

Down I went, wires in hand. Step... Another step. I felt my hamstring tense up. At this point, my entire leg and both arms began to quake again. There it went, my other hamstring locked. The pain was overbearing, intense. I began to pray that I would slip. If I passed out and fell through the ceiling, people would at the very *least* feign pity. However, I knew that if I passed out up there and had to be rescued... Friends and family were most assuredly going to make fun of me.

I'll take "Pity and Sympathy Casseroles" for $400.00 Alex.

Somewhere, at the other end of the cell signal, in another land of brighter, lighter days and happy children, I heard The Griz calling my name. I snapped back to attention. My chest was tight. I ripped the dusk mask off. I came to my senses. I didn't want to die up there alone! I poked the wires through the pre-drilled hole. The Griz grabbed them.

Then I recognized the full scope of my predicament. My legs were locked. I was experiencing intense pain. It was hot. My hands were slick with sweat and shaking uncontrollably. I was perched, spread eagled with one leg on each beam in the stupid attic, suspended above our stupid fireplace. I was positioned head pointed downwards towards the tiny little, hot pink dust bunny covered corner.

It was in that very moment that I realized, I don't even need surround sound. Nobody does. It's a useless luxury. I don't even like movies, or speakers. At that moment in my life, I was fully aware that I hated electricity, and modern conveniences. I loathed technology and the comforts of suburbia. I wanted to live in a tree house, but not a regular tree house. I wanted a tree house that wasn't up high. I wanted a tree house on the ground, with no cable, no attic, and no stupid surround sound.

I began to back out. *Slooowwwwly...* I was blocking out the heat, the sound of my husband's voice, the cramps, the nausea. I ordered myself back from whence I came. The moose, realizing the foolishness of hula hooping.

I survived the ascent back over the top of the fire place and back down to the main beam in the attic. I thought for a moment about abandoning our broom after I realized I forgot it over the stone fireplace. I remembered that I didn't have another to replace it, and I didn't want to be foolish. Two steps back, and I grabbed it. I was cramping and asthmatic, but who wastes money on a second broom?

I got stuck once during the process of the turnaround. I won't go into complete detail, but trust me... It wasn't pretty. Think hips. Think about that moose again, this time as he tries to squeeze through a mouse hole.

The headlamp was at that point dangling from a bun gone wild. There was sweating and dripping. My hands were shaking. My thighs were screaming. One more step. One more. Down the escape hatch onto solid flooring.

I made it down alive.

I've never come down a ladder so shakily. I got to the bottom and curled up on the floor at the foot of our bed. I was covered in fuzzy pink fiberglass shavings, sweating like a hooker on the front row of a Baptist outdoor holy tent Revival in the August heat.

My husband came back to check on me.

I asked for a few minutes to compose myself. He smiled that knowing smile and granted it. I must give him props and admit that he didn't take that moment to revel in my near-death experience or say, "I told you so."

I took a shower. I drank water until I thought I'd pop. I completed my day.

And I'm taking a moment to state in print. If we ever move, the surround sound stays. Either that or we're taking the whole stupid living room with us.

I'm not disconnecting... adding... updating... or re-placing wires. I'm not re-setting, removing, adding to or subtracting from what is already installed. I'm not kidding.

I'm not ever going up there again.

~~~ ★ ~~~

Parenting Survival Tip # 3: Don't ask questions. You really *REALLY* don't want to know.

I just yelled down the hall, "Captain A! Get out of my room. It's not a play area!"

He nonchalantly walked out, closing the door behind him. "I was talking to Batman mom. I'm done now."

He then casually strolled off to play. What ... What just happened???

~~~ ★ ~~~

Parenting Survival Tip # 68: Cherish your spouse. Without whom, it could have been you.

Pulling over in the car... Three minutes.

Hearing your son whine that he needs go "frow up"... Four minutes.

Unbuckling the car seat... Thirty seconds.

Seeing the look on your husband's face when he's standing outside, willing to help, and the child announces he doesn't need to "frow up," but rather needs to poop in the leaves on the side of the road... *PRICELESS.*

~~~ ★ ~~~

Parenting Survival Tip # 69: It's not logical... But sometimes it's just funny.

B-Dubya: I know how to make glow in the dark nail polish. I want to try it.

Me: You just cut a glow in the dark bracelet and pour it into your polish.

B-Dubya: (smugly) Yeah, but do you know what color polish you have to use?

Me: (smugly in return) Clear. Annnnnd your fingers would only glow for one night.

B-Dubya: *Unless you slept with your hand in the freezer!*

#KillShot
#ShesAGenius
#YaGotMeThere

~~~ ★ ~~~

Parenting Survival Tip # 70: They're honest... Painfully honest.

Captain A: *Awwwww.* I was peeling that doubled (deviled) egg, and I messed up the white stuff momma... I'm *soooo* sorry.

Me: No worries son. This whole batch looks awful. Look at the ones I did before you got in here.

Captain A: (looking down at the pan of mangled eggs) Wow Momma. That's *terrible.* You peeled those eggs pitiful. I guess I didn't do so bad.

Me: Thanks son. Get outta my kitchen.

~~~ ★ ~~~

Parenting Survival Tip # 71: Vegetables can stir up panic.

Honey Badger: *TOMATO! A TOMATO* outside. *TOMAAAAA AATO!*

Me: No son. It's thunder. Not a tornado.
Honey Badger: Ummmm. Oh.

~~~ ★ ~~~

Parenting Survival Tip # 72: They do love you. They do. They really do.

Me: (writhing in pain with a Charlie horse in my thigh after bending down to tuck my kids in) *Oh! A cramp! A cramp in my leg! Give me a minute! Give me a minute!*
B-Dubya: (matter-of-factly and without a smidgen of compassion) Be thankful you aren't swimming in over six feet of water.
Captain A: (nonchalantly) Yes. 'Cause you'd be already dead Momma.

~~~ ★ ~~~

Parenting Survival Tip # 73: Remember that sometimes, boys really do care about your things getting ruined... *Sometimes.*

Captain A: My feet are *disgusting.* Can I scrub them?
Me: Take a wash cloth and wet it. Use soap. Scrub your feet. Hurry up. It's bedtime.

He chooses a ninja turtle wash cloth, and off he goes to the bathroom. A few minutes later, I hear a hesitant and worried voice from the bathroom.

Captain A: Moooooooom! The dirt is getting on the wash cloth.
Me: That's the whole point son.

#FacePalm
#RocketScientist

~~~ ★ ~~~

Parenting Survival Tip # 74: Make the best of it. Keep it real.

After I fussed for the second time about Captain A sitting in his seat in the car with his knees up under him, his daddy chimed in.

The Griz: Boy, you better sit in that seat like you've got some sense. I know you don't have any. But just... Pretend like you do.

~~~ ★ ~~~

Parenting Survival Tip # 75: Always keep extra can openers on hand.

Have you ever...
Needed coffee...
And realized that you were out of creamer...
And been *ecstatic* to find that you had *allllllll* the ingredients to make homemade creamer...
And then in your haste to make a sandwich for your daughter, you left the can opener down where Wreck-It-Ralph (the two-year-old, aka Honey Badger) could get his grubby little hands on it?
So you come back from sandwich making...
Only to realize that your can opener...
The one that opened a can of evaporated milk two seconds earlier...

That can opener...

It's not working anymore...

It's a hand turned can opener, nothing fancy. It's just a can normal can opener.

It's been on the planet probably since the 70's. It should be bulletproof.

So instead of using the aforementioned can opener, you ponder loudly while shooting daggers out of your face at Wreck-It-Ralph... *HOW DO YOU EVEN BREAK ONE OF THOSE!?!*

You *seriously* contemplate chewing through the lid on the condensed milk...

And then you shoot more daggers...

And Wreck-It-Ralph walks through the kitchen and says, "What doing?"

And in frustration... You jam the can opener on the can and twist the wrong direction...

And...

It works!!!!!

So you open the can... The wrong way...

And then you sit down with hot coffee... and homemade creamer...

And a broken can opener...

And an unapologetic Wreck-It--Ralph...

And you know that today is going to be an EPIC day...

Have you ever done that?

Me neither.

~~~ ★ ~~~

# Day 11

A memory from December 2010:

*"Moooooooommmmm..."*

This isn't a normal yell.

I go running.

I find her in her room. She's pointing at her dresser.

"Ants." She yells. "Where's dad? They're back. Where's dad?" She's panicking. There's a trail of the little monsters marching around.

I think to myself, "*Helloooo...* I can kill ants."

I want her to understand that regardless the circumstance, I'll try to fix it. I say quietly, "Daddy isn't here, but I can help."

"But Mom, they're ants." She isn't giving in. "Where's Dad?"

"He's at the post office." I reply. I'm starting to get perturbed by this point. I can kill ants. I gave birth to you. I wiped your backside for years. I successfully kept you alive before I even met

The Griz, and I've managed to feed this entire family for two years now. I can handle an ant.

In walks the little fat boy. "Bug." He states matter-of-factly. One syllable. No nonsense, he cut straight to the chase. Toddlers are very precise.

Off B-Dubya goes again. She's on a mission. "Where's Dad?"

"He's running errands, and I can handle this." He's not here. Why is that such a big deal? I can kill ants.

"Bug." The toddler and his one syllable again, clarifying that he's on scene, qualified, and ready to supervise.

"Thank you Captain A for the observation. They *are* bugs."

"*Mooooooooooooooom...*" nasally, whiney, overkill on drama voice emerges. "Don't kill them all. Just smush most of them. I want to study one. I need to learn. I need to see how he lives."

I slowly and firmly tell B-Dubya that I'm not leaving ants alive for her to keep as pets. Not a single one if I can help it. They have overrun our house. We've called the exterminators. The bug specialists have come out three times now. They sent an "ant specialist" out here too. Thanks to him... We still have ants. I ponder if all "specialists" are as proficient as he, and if they're able to keep a job too. I could SURELY be just as deficient as they! Why am I not getting paid?

The ants still show up unannounced, unwelcomed, and unashamed. They march around our house. I must admit that I'm thankful that when they came to this rally, at LEAST they gave me the dignity of leaving their pom-poms and picket signs at home.

They march around dumb stuff:

> The washing machine.
> Our laundry hamper.
> The changing table.
> And today, they were marching around a book on B-Dubya's dresser.

They were just marching... Endless marching... Lines of filthy little trespassers.

"Bug." The toddler is back. Not just back, but stepping confidently into his role of supervising and informing.

"Yes Captain A. It's a bug." This repetition would be comical, if it was happening to someone else. I keep on steady smushing, crushing, whatever I can do to maim and kill.

"Where's Daddy?" Here she goes again. The child is incessant and apparently convinced of my inability to hold down the fort in this battle. "Where's Daddy? He'll use the chemical stuff."

"Chemicals are bad for you." I tried to divert her one-track focus. "I can handle this. Daddy will be home soon. Don't worry. B-Dubya... It's okay."

"Bug." I hear the one syllable word again. It's forceful, informative. He's standing behind me. He won't give up.

I'm *trying* to keep it together. This is ridiculous. "Yes son. It's a bug. I see them. They're bugs. I'm killing them. Give me a moment."

"Mom." B-Dubya lets out a frustrated sigh. "Ants are stupid. I don't know why they come in my room."

"B-Dubya. That's a bad word. Don't say that."

"But you tell daddy ants are stupid." She has a valid point. "And they come in the house and do stupid things and they won't go away."

Touché little girl... Touché.

"It's a bad word for me too. I'm sorry I set a bad example. Don't say that word."

"Ant." The toddler again, he's still informing me on the crisis. Now he swaps it up. He narrows the gap in vocabulary. He needs to make sure I know that we're dealing with a menace. There is depth and gravity coming from the 20-month-old. He means business.

"Yes, Captain A. It's an ant. Good job. Now go away." I love him. I do. But good heavens, I recognize it's an ant! He's announced it. I got the memo... and the fax... and the airplane fly over with banner.

He marches out of the room and down the hall. I make the mistake of thinking I'm in the clear.

B-Dubya is intently searching for something that she can't seem to find. "Mom. Where's my glass? You know, the one that makes things look bigger. Don't squish that one!!! Moooom... Why did you squish it? I told you not to!!!!"

"B-Dubya," I say calmly. "We can't keep one alive. They have chemicals on their bodies that leave a trail behind so that other ants can find your dresser."

"*Ewwwwwww!*" She's shocked and horrified. "That's gross. I need to go wash my hands! You can squish them all now." She said this as though she had given me permission... To kill ants in my own house.

The toddler returns from down the hall. I pay him no mind, but I do notice he has a book in his hand. It's a board book of the Alphabet, a first words for toddlers type book. He purposely opens it to page one. It's letter "A". He points to the page.

"Ant." He says clearly. I turn and look. Sure enough. There's a little illustrated 6-legged arthropod on the page.

"Yes. Captain A... I see. They're ants. Thanks for clarifying." I don't know why I'm encouraging him. But his tenacity is noteworthy. Just in case I didn't understand "bug" and "ant"... Now I have a picture to compare the menace to. You're so helpful.

B-Dubya studies her dresser. She surveys my work. She evidently approves. "Whew!" She sighs as if a great weight has lifted from her miniature shoulders. "They're dead. Thanks mom."

"Ant." He's still pointing at the book. He's still clarifying. He's still supervising and informing.

We somehow survived the Great Ant Invasion of 2010.

And the next time I see the "bug-man-ant specialist guy"... I'm kicking him in the shins, stealing his badge, and taking his job.

~~~ ★ ~~~

Parenting Survival Tip # 76: Assume it was a compliment. Kids don't see the world the same way adults do.

Captain A: B-Dubya, you're very beautiful. You have skinny legs.
    But ummmm... You do have chonky thighs.
B-Dubya: Thanks Captain A. I get those from mom.

Not sure if that was a compliment, but I'll take it. And I'll pretend not to be offended. At least the kids are good at encouraging each other, and they have a healthy view of body image and silver linings ... even in "chonky-ness".

~~~ ★ ~~~

Parenting Survival Tip # 77: Just listen. Sometimes they need that too.

I was a little sentimental today while I was looking at my six-year-old.

Me: Ya know sometimes I look at you... And your sister... And your brother...

Captain A: (interrupting) And we look like ogres?

Me: No son. I look at you, and I know God must love me a lot... Because He let me be your mom.

Captain A: Well. We also look like ogres.

Me: Yeah. Sometimes.

Captain A: I like honey bees. They're cute.

Me: Me too.

Captain A: I like honey.

Me: Me too.

Captain A: You know, honey is bee barf mom. Dad told me.

Me: *What???*

Captain A: It's bee barf.

Me: That's gross.

Captain A: But it tastes good. (long reflective pause) Mom. I wish... I wish human barf tasted good. But it doesn't.

#Reflections
#DeepThoughts
#LifeWithBoys


~~~ ★ ~~~


Parenting Survival Tip # 78: You MUST be precise.

Hearing a drawer open behind me and knowing said drawer contains scissors and screwdrivers and such...

Me: What are you getting into son?

Captain A: A drawer.

Me: But son, what are you getting in there for?

Captain A: Only for a minute.

Me: *For... The... Love...* (clearly specifying now) What are you getting out of the drawer????

Captain A: Oh... Just a pencil.

~~~ ★ ~~~

Parenting Survival Tip # 79. Their 'help' is your mess, but they're trying.

Captain A just wants to be a big boy and help. I prepped my coffee pot last night, so this morning I ask him to go push the button. Nothing else. Just push the button.

He comes back proudly sauntering. "I put water in that glass thing...*Then* I pushed the button Momma. You're welcome Momma. I did it juuust for you." In my slow-motion movie voice in my waking stupor. *"Noooooooooooooooooooo!!!!!!!"*

~~~ ★ ~~~

Parenting Survival Tip # 80. It's close. Soooooo close.

Me: What did you guys eat for dinner when you went out with Ms. Kim?

B-Dubya: I ate noodles, and my eggroll is left over. You can have it.

Captain A: I ate Siamese chicken. But it's mine. You can't have it. You can have B-Dubya's noodles though.

Me: What exactly is Siamese chicken?

Captain A: It's a chicken. It's a red red chicken.

Me: I don't even like anything Siamese. So, I'm cool with that.

~~~ ★ ~~~

Parenting Survival Tip # 52: Just smile and wave boys, smile and wave.

I wonder if Honey Badger realizes that in a dire emergency... It's *probably* easier to run to the potty if he either:

A. Takes his undies *completely* off before running.
  Or
B. Leaves them pulled up until he gets to the bathroom.

The terrified waddle of impending doom that I just witnessed shuffling towards the bathroom was utterly ridiculous... A train wreck.

~~~ ★ ~~~

Parenting Survival Tip # 81: Life lessons will be shared.

Captain A: Look B-Dubya. Listen. There is *two* ways your body can burp. One way, (pauses for dramatic effect) Comes out your mouth.

It's at this point that my mother instinct kicks in, and my ears shut down. I can't even handle the wisdom coming from our back seat on this ride home.

~~~ ★ ~~~

Parenting Survival Tip # 82: There's always one who will appreciate the little things. The others will be mad at that one. Always.

The Griz: (very frustrated) B-Dubya and Captain A, get a trash bag and get your rears outside and clean out the back seat of the car where you've left all your trash... Again.

B-Dubya & Captain A: (simultaneously downcast and dejectedly compliant) Yes sir.

Honey Badger: (very excited and missing the gravity of the situation entirely) *Oooohhhhh!* Daddy! Daddy! Can I take my rear outside? Can I take my rear outside too Daddy???!!!

~~~ ★ ~~~

# Day 12

A memory from January 2011:

Tonight, as I tucked my daughter in and said our prayers, I was blessed by her little voice coming out from the depths of the Dora the Explorer Tent set up on her bed. I remembered as much as I could so that you could share my blessing.

Dear God:

Thank you for this day.

Thank you for my family and my brother.

Thank you for our house and our babysitter and letting her go home today.

Thank you for the snow (dramatic and confused pause) No. Thank you, even though it wasn't snow. It was crunchy stuff.

Thank you for our house.

And Lord... Please let us sleep well. No bad dreams tonight.

Thank you for our dinner and for cake.

Thank you for our friends. And thank you for Cortney, and for Corey, and for our grandparents.

And Lord... Please no bad dreams tonight. This is very important!

Lord thank you for our house.

And please be with us to keep out the cold air and the ants.

Please let the ants eat our bait. Draw them *cloooooser* to you Lord. I know they're your creatures too, but ants are crazy. And they're dumb. And they keep coming into our house. And this behavior is unnecessary. So Lord. Be with them. Help them die.

And Lord... (she took a deep breath) Thank you for my baby that mommy will have soon. And this time... Let it be a baby girl... So I can do her hair.

(Pause: Don't even think it... The answer is... NO! I'm not. And not planning on it. The end!)

And I've mentioned this several times. But it's very important. One more time. I know you don't mind hearing me. We need good sleep tonight. Please let us have no bad dreams.

Lord... Thank you for everything you've given us.

Thank you for my brother, even though he drools. He loves you too.

Help us to be Your light.

And all these things we ask in Jesus' precious name we pray... Amen.

I don't know about anything else, but I know that I want the faith and sincerity of that child. I want to say a simple prayer. I want to believe it. That's my desire.

~~~ ★ ~~~

Parenting Survival Tip # 83: Keep your trash cans clean, and your laughter inaudible.

Captain A had a night terror. The Griz got him up and directed him into our bathroom. We were in the middle of a discussion when Captain A came through our bedroom. He was sleep walking to go potty.

It's normal. It happens a lot here.

Don't ask.

I warned The Griz, "Keep an eye on him. Last night he tried to climb into the bathtub."

The Griz nonchalantly told me, "He's fine. He's just scratching his belly."

We continued talking. Then I hear... "Captain A! *Stop! Ugh! Quit...Stop! No! In the toilet! Pee in the toilet son. IN THE TOILET!"*

*#ItWasAccidental*

*#AtLeastHeHadGoodAim*
*#GladITookOutTheTrashToday*
*#LifeWithBoys*

~~~ ★ ~~~

Parenting Survival Tip # 84: If you haven't thought it as a parent, you're not trying hard enough.

Actual conversation between my husband and I:

The Griz: If I were an animal, I'd *seriously* consider eating the kids.
Me: I'm *not* an animal. I've totally considered it.

~~~ ★ ~~~

Parenting Survival Tip # 85: There is ALWAYS a loophole, and boys will ALWAYS find it.

The Griz had some place to go this morning. I'm laying here in the dark. My door opens, and the bed shakes. It's obvious I've been visited by one of my children.

A small whisper breaks the silence as I smile. "Morning Momma. Daddy said not to come back here and talk to you."

So, I ask the logical question, "Then why are you here son?"

"Well. I just love you. Annnnd I wanted to know if I could play a game on the Xbox." Captain A's logic is error free.

"So you didn't come back here to talk to me?" I asked.

The little whispered voice, matter-of-factly replied, "Nope. Just to ask you a question."

I gave him permission, and he slid down off the bed. My door closed as I listened to little footsteps down the hall.

They're knuckleheads. But they're mine.

~~~ ★ ~~~

Parenting Survival Tip # 86: Let them test things when they insist. They learn that way.

Upon finding the chicken bouillon can that I had just accidentally dropped in the floor.

Captain A: Momma, I want some. What is that stuff?
Me: It's something I sometimes use when I cook to season stuff and make it taste better. You can't have it straight. You won't like it.
Captain A: I'mma sniff it. I want some.
Me: Fine. Go ahead and sniff it. Tell me what you think.
Captain A: (inhaling deeply) Mmmmmmmm. It smells... It smells... It smells a little bit like good. Annnnnnd a little bit like dog food too.

~~~ ★ ~~~

Parenting Survival Tip # 87: Sometimes it doesn't make sense. But it does make for good stories.

I walked into the bathroom today to get ready to go to church.

My five-year-old was in there, and he was going potty.

He wasn't going potty like a "normal" five-year-old.

No.

He had decided that the best way to save time and energy was to go potty *without* unzipping his pants.

Not only did he *not* waste two seconds unzipping. He also saved some precious nanoseconds by choosing to also keep his jeans up... and *firmly* in place.

Extremely efficient.

Now, I have to give him credit. He did *indeed* let the toilet seat up as he has been trained.

However...

I walked in to see him stretching and straining in order to save the two seconds it would have taken to release his zipper.

Again... That would make entirely too much sense.

So he stretches... and strains... and gets it juuuuuust far enough out that he arches.....*ARCHES!* Managing somehow to pee down the *back* of the lid of the toilet... Narrowly missing the handle... And also, narrowly avoiding my wall... And the toilet paper roll holder.

I. Am. Horrified.

I'm also silently stunned by this master of ingenuity.

Me: *SON, WHAT IN THE WORLD ARE YOU DOING? WHY DIDN'T YOU JUST UNZIP YOUR PANTS?!?!?!*
Captain A: (mouth agape) Mom! You saw that right? Wasn't that *amazing*?
Me: Yes. Yes son. It was incredible. Now clean up my bathroom.

~~~ ★ ~~~

Parenting Survival Tip # 88: Everything is a technicality. *Everything.*

Captain A: *STOP IT! DON'T HIT ME!*
B-Dubya: You hit me first.
Captain A: *I didn't hit you! I PUNCHED you!!!*

~~~ ★ ~~~

Parenting Survival Tip # 89: They listen carefully. Ohhhhh so carefully.

Captain A: Daddy. Does your leg hurt you?
The Griz: Yes.
Captain A: Daddy. Does your back hurt?
The Griz: Yes. It does.
Captain A: So Daddy... Is your bladder hurting?
[me silently choking on my spit and laughing]
The Griz: No. My bladder is fine.

Captain A: That woman asked you about your bladder.

[HOLD THE PHONE! Whhhhhhattttttttttt?]

The Griz: Yes… At the chiropractor, the lady asked about my bladder function. But it's fine. I promise.

~~~ ★ ~~~

Parenting Survival Tip # 90: Their priorities *will* differ from yours, and that's okay.

Bedtime prayers…

Captain A: Dear God. Thank you for this day that you have given. Please let there be no bad weather. Please tomorrow let us ride the four-wheeler and catch the cat. And then can we go to Egypt… But we don't want to see the fighting. But Lord I want to see mummies. But don't let them chase me. Amen.

~~~ ★ ~~~

# Day 13

A memory from December, 2010:

There are times I miss being single.

There are times I miss the freedom of staying up late. I miss sleeping late. I miss eating Ramen noodles and not having to cook for others.

But...

If I was single without children...

I would never know what it's like to hold a sleeping part of my own heart in my arms.

I would never know the peace of watching my kids play together.

I would never have the completion I feel at the end of a long day with my husband fed... the laundry done... and the kids snoring soundly.

I would never know the feeling of having a Tonka dump truck climbing up my leg (complete with backing up beeping noises) while I'm trying to get into the bathroom in an emergency situation. (I completed my mission FYI... the beeping dump truck joined me. We were a rescue duo.)

I would never have had the opportunity to experience a Japanese Steakhouse to the fullest, as I did yesterday. I dined with two of the most important people in my life.

We had our company Christmas dinner yesterday. Our section at work got to choose the restaurant we went to. We met at 11:30 AM and had lunch together. It's a great group of people. I enjoy their company. My job is good. My God is better. I'm blessed.

Now before I get into the heart of my story, I must preface this.

From the day I met my incredible husband, he has been clear about a few things in his life.

Number one... There are a few things you will never catch him doing.

1. Skydiving.
2. Mountain Climbing in the snow
3. Surfing.
4. Bungee Jumping.

Or anything else that "only crazy white people do" that could cause death. He's made it clear. Being safety oriented is genetic. It's part of his culture to self-preserve. He won't do anything for a thrill that could end in spontaneous combustion... Intestinal spillage... Or a splattering sound made by his body. No skiing... No swimming with sharks... No storm chasing... Period. The end.

The second thing that he's made abundantly clear is this:

*If you see me running... It's not for pleasure... It's because there is something bad about to happen...Something is not right...If I'm running... You better run too. Or you will be left alone with whatever that bad thing is... If you see me running... And you don't join... You're on your own.*

Clear.
Double check.
I'm on it.

I've heard of at least one instance where he left a chick he was dating in the woods in the mountains by herself when he heard something growl. My husband is chivalrous. He's amazing. He's a great father and protector. But if it comes to being eaten by an unseen wild animal... He's out.

So with that being said, we go back to our regularly scheduled programming.

The Japanese Restaurant.

I thought the experience would be fun. I thought the kids would enjoy someone cooking at the table in front of them. I was kinda right. Mostly. Well… I was a little right.

We got to the restaurant. We checked in with our group.

B-Dubya introduced herself to everyone in the party... and the restaurant... and the world.

Captain A promptly found a seat in the lap of an unsuspecting, yet willing co-worker. We were ready to go.

Our appetizers came out.

I ordered sushi. I've discovered a love for it from my hubs, who has an amazing sense of taste about food.

The lady sitting next to B-Dubya ordered tempura battered, deep fried veggies.

She and B-Dubya began to chow down.

I told B-Dubya at least twice to stop taking this lady's food. We have our own food coming.

I kept turning around and seeing more veggies on her plate.

It wasn't until about the third time I reprimanded my daughter that I realized my co-worker was waiting until I turned my head and sticking more bites on B-Dubya's plate. And how can I get mad about that?

*"Stop putting vegetables on my child's plate!"*

That even sounded stupid. I didn't say it.

I gave up. Eat your veggies... or her veggies... whatever... I don't care.

Captain A had seen I had food. He came back to join me rather quickly.

I placed him in his chair.

The chef came, and I'll admit, I got excited. Oh yeah! It was showtime!

He had on a tall hat, and he was loud. The kids were intrigued.

The cooking began.

Those men are so talented! This one was banging his spatulas. He was flipping...twisting... turning... popping... clanging... banging...cracking eggs... tossing veggies.

B-Dubya was enamored. She was watching raptly, slack jawed.

Captain A was the polar opposite. He was completely unimpressed. He was sucking his pacifier with a vengeance. His eyebrows were furrowed. My toddler was probably wondering why this idiot wasn't getting a spankin' for all the noise he was making in public. He must not have been raised by a mean mom.

The chef then poured the oil on the Hibachi grill.

He spread it. Poured it. Built a tower of onions... Annnnd lit it on fire.

I feel the heat. I sense the excitement. I'm thrilled. B-Dubya squeals. I understand her happiness.

From the high chair, I hear Captain A say... "Hot." Clear. Concise. One syllable.

I look over at B-Dubya... In the flare from the fire... Her eyes twinkle. "*WHHHOOOA!*" she says. "This is so cool!"

I look over for Captain A's response.

He's gone.

He's twisted around in his high chair... Attempting a Houdini style escape from the box of death. He's literally doing everything he can to make a quick exit.

Had I given him time... He and his paci would have gotten down... stolen my keys... buckled up in the car... threw it into drive and left me and B-Dubya in the Japanese Steakhouse to fend for ourselves.

In that moment... I saw The Griz.

Me and B-Dubya were having a blast... Excited in the moment... The flames... The sights. The smells... The sounds.

Captain A was having none of it.

The building was going up in flames... and we were too dumb to see it.

He instantly turned into his father, and though he only speaks a few words clearly... I hear him loud and clear.

"You crazy white women can stay in this burning building if you want to. But something's not right. I'm out. And if you see me running and you don't join me... You're on your own."

~~~ ★ ~~~

Parenting Survival Tip # 91. Little brother antics are timeless. Sometimes the entertainment lies in not stopping them.

I just heard a muffled. "*Let me ooooouuuuuuut!*"

It sounded panicked. It was most definitely Captain A. It sounded like he was in a box... Or locked in the closet. I waited.

I then heard B-Dubya say, "Seriously?"

A few moments later, Captain A appeared in my room. He was slightly disheveled.

"Son, what just happened?" I asked.

He sheepishly looked at the floor. "Well B-Dubya was watching YouTube in her room, and I wanted to see. So, I hid under the bed. And I waited. Well..." A long pause and sigh ensued. I'm not sure if it was for dramatic effect, or because he was aware of how ridiculous the rest of the story would be. "Weeeeeell.... She was only watching stupid American girl videos, and I wanted out from under the stupid bed. So, I turned my head to leave. But there was this huge metal bar and well... My head kind of got stuck. And I needed help. It was scary."

I can't stop laughing. His cranium... Is huuuuge. I hope he learned a lesson.

#LifeWithBoys

#ClassicLittleBrother
#TheMetalBarAintBig
#ItsYourSkull
#FacePalm

~~~ ★ ~~~

Parenting Survival Tip # 3: Don't ask questions. You really *REALLY* don't want to know.

Me: Hey dude, that Hershey Kiss over there is yours. Your brother and sister already had one.
Captain A: Oh! That's great! I'm so glad... Because I got sanitizer in my mouth a few hours ago. This will *definitely* help.

~~~ ★ ~~~

Parenting Survival Tip # 92: There's never really peace and quiet. It's *always* just the calm before the storm.

As I was typing today, Honey Badger ran through my room sans underwear... Again.

He stopped and grabbed a paintbrush. He then ran into the bathroom. After a brief pause, he yelled for help. Because according to him, "I *need* to poop in here quick! But I can't climb up because I'm too *little*! *Heeeeeeeellllllpppppp!*"

Then, when it was all over, he said, "You're welcome!" And then he ran out to put on his Batman underwear.

It's not quiet here. It's not uneventful. It's still perfect.

~~~ ★ ~~~

Parenting Survival Tip #167: Theology does NOT trump naptime.

Me: Son. We're making slime today. If you wanna make slime, you *must* take a nap. No exceptions.

Captain A: But...

Me: No buts. Go lay down. You *must* take a nap if you wanna make slime.

Captain A: But what about B-Dubya? Is she going to sleep and make slime?

Me: Yes.

Captain A: But what if she sleeps and I don't?

Me: Then she chooses to make slime and you choose not to.

Captain A: Well... What if I lay down and I try to sleep and God speaks?

Me: *Seriously*? Go to bed.

Captain A: God speaks. And when he does... He says he doesn't like not fair stuff. You hafta do fair stuff. That's what God says makes him happy.

Me: Go to bed son. Your theology is all off kilter. Sleep will fix that.

~~~ ★ ~~~

Parenting Survival Tip # 94: Your faith will reach them, and they'll definitely misinterpret it.

I set plates on the table for dinner tonight. I had baked lasagna and toasted garlic bread.

Captain A: Ohhhhhh bread! (pauses in deep thought) Wait... Is this the bread of idleness?

What in the world?

~~~ ★ ~~~

Parenting Survival Tip # 95: Life advice is so much better coming from a child.

B-Dubya: (giving deep advice to her brother) One time I had a blister, and I peeled it. And it *hurt*. So bad... *LIKE SOOO BAD*. Never do that. *Never...* I mean... I've never had a baby... But I'm sure it hurt like that.

[Yep... childbirth is *exactly* like that.]

~~~ ★ ~~~

Parenting Survival Tip # 96: They're honest. Brutally, painfully honest.

Captain A: Momma... I just like Grandpa better... Because you... You're mean to little kids.

Parenting Survival Tip # 97: Check it before you put it in the microwave. *Always.*

Have you ever spent fifteen minutes of your life fanning doors in a quiet house with three children who are sleeping.... *Terrified* that the smoke alarm was going to sound and blare them all into horrified chaos at midnight... Because you opened the microwave after warming a rice heating pad... And smoke *billowed out.* And the whole house smelled like burnt rice. Have you ever realized that you fairly nearly burnt your ENTIRE neighborhood down... Because your twenty-two-month-old decided that he was done with his bubble gum and spit it out and affixed it to previously mentioned rice heating pad.

Yeah... Me neither.
#ThatJustHappened

~~~ ★ ~~~

# Day 14

A memory from August 2011:

"Mom... I need a pet."

Inward groan... We have two dogs and a two-year-old, and a plethora of dust bunnies. Doesn't that count for something?

"Mom... Mary Kate has one. She's gonna bring it to me."

Mary Kate must be in my daughter's first grade class. Mary Kate and I need to have a talk, as do Mary Kate's mom and I.

"Mom. She brought one to school today."

What in the??? What's going on at this school? Have they no rules?

"Mom...Mom... Mom... *Listen*... Don't look so worried. It's a tadpole... I need a tadpole. It's a perfect pet."

Me thinking quietly to myself... How in the world did this little girl bring a tadpole to school? This is gonna be good. I actually work up the courage to ask... "How?"

"Mom... She brought it in an orange juice bottle... But don't worry mom. She washed the orange juice out first. She brought it in her back pack."

Laugh out *LOUD*!

Scratch that original thought. Mary Kate and I don't have a care in the world. Now Mary Kate and her mother... that's a different story. I'm thinking her mother is in the dark about this whole "take a baby frog to school in an orange juice bottle" thing. I'm thinking me myself that I gave birth to a pretty cool kid... At least she asks before bringing home amphibians.

And I'm thinkin' that perhaps... My problems aren't such a big deal after all.

"Mom." She snaps me out of my daydream. "Mom, did you hear me? I can bring it home and feed it crickets... Tadpoles LOVE crickets... This is gonna be great."

To update you... I told her "No." I also informed her that tadpoles don't eat crickets... and they don't drink orange juice. But I did hug her, and I told her I love her.

Now... Your dogs... Go play with them. Ally and Wanda LOVE YOU!

If that doesn't satisfy... Go find a dust bunny... We have several... Thousand.

Or your brother... He's a cool pet. He fetches...And he would probably eat crickets... And he LOVES orange juice.

Sorry about the laughter Mrs. Mary Kate's mom... I can't help it.

*I FEEL YOUR PAIN!*

Now if I check my first grader's back pack over the weekend... And I find an orange juice bottle.... Me and you... We might have to have a face to face...

~~~ ★ ~~~

Parenting Survival Tip # 98: Get used to questioning your sanity.

Please get the dinosaur out of your ear son.

Yes... I just had to say that.

~~~ ★ ~~~

Parenting Survival Tip # 99: Remember that they're always learning, even when it seems impossible.

Honey Badger is currently upset with his sister. Apparently, our trip to the fair was productive. It impacted him deeply.

When she began to make eggs this morning, she caught a full out lecture from the three-year-old about the evils of eating 'baby shickens'.

He's *not* ok with that.

~~~ ★ ~~~

Parenting Survival Tip # 100: Time is only measured in *your* world, not theirs.

What ranks up at the top with a root canal and gall stones?

Watching a three-year-old who demands independence, trying to redress himself in inside out footie pajamas. It's especially painful when he *insists* on doing it without assistance.

It's excruciating...
It's taking forever...
It's currently been 11 minutes...
He ain't done...
I ain't gonna make it.

~~~ ★ ~~~

Parenting Survival Tip # 101: They're gross. They just are. It's not your fault. It's a design flaw.

Honey Badger: I need some mustard! (pronounced "mus-therd")
Me: Son you're eating a grilled cheese sandwich. You don't need mustard. Do you need ketchup?
Honey Badger: Yes-th. I need ketchup for my apples. And ketchup for my pickle.

~~~ ★ ~~~

Parenting Survival Tip # 102: Know your scream pitches. Is it serious?

Upon hearing the littlest yell, and ascertaining that it's not a life/death yell... I send the journalist on a mission to review and bring back her account.

Me: B-Dubya, please go check on your baby brother and report back.

She runs down the hall. Promptly returning. She's breathless, but unflustered.

Me: B-Dubya. Dear. Why did he yell? What is happening?
B-Dubya: Oh. It's nothing. The boys are sword fighting again... Honey Badger died... Again.
As she's reporting, there's another yell...
B-Dubya: Annnnnd again.

~~~ ★ ~~~

# Day 15

Sitting and listening to the rain... I admit I'm terrified by the ferocity of the lightning.

My hubs just joined me in the living room.

He said he doesn't want to die in our bathroom while getting ready to take a shower. This would make a terrible obituary.

Although funny... It would be terrible.

He was shaving. He said the lightning struck, and the thunder happened simultaneously... And he almost cut his jugular vein. And he thought a pine tree landed on the house.

It didn't.

And now he's standing out here looking at me. And we're discussing what we do if our house gets struck by lightning.

Here's the plan.

He's the only one in our house who knows where his keys are. Ever.

Mine are perpetually lost... Along with the matches of 63 pairs of socks and my original name badge from GEICO.

I'm worthless.

So in this plan, it's his job to grab the keys and Captain A.

I grab B-Dubya.

I have no idea who grabs my hubby's clothes. Because it's my job to grab the safe...And it's not my fault he's just in shorts.

He's gonna be cold and wet... and angry about it. But in my defense, I didn't agree to that in our vows.

"To have and to hold... For better or for worse... For richer or for poorer...And I'll grab your clothes outta the bedroom in the event our house gets hit by lightning while you're shaving and preparing to take a shower..."

Um... Nope. Not in the vows.

What to save in the event of a fire... What to leave...

Definitely the kids and the safe come.

It's a safe, but not because we have anything of value. It just contains paperwork that proves we're real people, United States citizens, and we don't have rabies or tetanus and such. You know? Essentials.

And then we thought about our television. It was a gift. Probably the only thing of value we own. And then I thought about all of my drawings... Hours of work...And yeah... I'm just praying we don't get hit because we might burn up trying to grab dumb stuff that's already insured.

I'm praying this storm is fast moving. I'm tired and I need to go to bed, and I need to take a shower too... And my hubs is afraid of a tree falling through the roof.

I am too.

But I'm not as afraid of trees as I am of getting electrocuted while in the shower.

That would stink too.

Obit would read:

Was found in a bathtub... alone and abandoned... Her husband and two children were in the front yard. Husband had a horrendous cut from shaving... and he was wearing only his shorts. He was angry. The children looked confused. The woman appeared to have tinkled on herself a little when she realized taking a shower during the storm was a foolish idea. Her assumption was correct. The end.

Whew! In the time it's taken me to write this... The storm has passed.

It's quiet now, and the rain has almost stopped.

And I should probably check on the dogs, but they'll stomple me to death if I open the back door. (Stomple: verb; to stomp upon in the course of trampling)

Yet another horrible way to die.

Stompled by mutt dogs in the aftermath of a severe thunderstorm. Local area woman found with a paw print on her forehead.

On that note, with the lightening in the distance I'll risk electrocution. I'll go take a shower to prep for bed.

Thank you and good night.

~~~ ★ ~~~

Parenting Survival Tip # 103: The younger ones WILL exact their revenge on the older ones. Just give it time. It's *well* worth the wait.

The Griz and I are in the living room. The boys are down the hall, taking a bath with Minion banana bath wash and bubbles.

Honey Badger: (singing) P... P.... P.. P. PPPPPPPPPPPP... P. P. Peeeeeeeeeeeee!
Captain A: (gravely serious) Honey Badger... Did you just pee in the water?
Honey Badger: (suspicious silence)
Captain A: I'm for real. *Did you pee in the water?*
Honey Badger: (mischievously) Uhhhhhhhh... Nope.

Captain A: (talking through his teeth now, hissing his worry) I'm *sooo* serious. Honey Badger... Are you telling the truth? Did you pee in the water?

Honey Badger: (still singing) Nooooo-*ooohhhhh*! And I'm not getting *ouuuuuuuut*!

Captain A: MOOOOOOOOOMMMMM! Honey Badger won't get out of the tub, and he needs to potty!

Honey Badger: (whispering) *Noooooooooo*!

I'm seriously dying here. I can't laugh out loud, but I understand Captain A's concern. I'd be worried too. I have to stifle a giggle as they whisper fight over who needs to potty and who needs to be quiet. I calmly command Honey Badger to disembark from the tub. I wait expectantly. I'm hoping that he *does* pee in the potty because that's the only way to ensure he hasn't peed in the tub already with the angry six-year-old.

I hear it. Whhhheeeewwww! He did indeed *need* to potty. Relief was had by all. And Captain A has *no idea* how much joy I took away from his plight.

~~~ ★ ~~~

Parenting Survival Tip # 104: They'll get it right, eventually.

Me: Son... You're slower than molasses.

Captain A: WHOOAAAA!!! That's slow!!!

B-Dubya: I know what molasses are! That's a disease!

#ApplyingKnowledge
#You'reDoingItRight.

~~~ ★ ~~~

Parenting Survival Tip # 105: Enjoy them while they're little. It won't be gross forever.

Captain A: (while eating a hamburger and watching Frozen in Italian with English subtitles) When people kiss each other on the mouth... That's unacceptable and *totally* disgusting.

~~~ ★ ~~~

Parenting Survival Tip # 106: Imagination is only safe to a certain point.

As I'm putting on my makeup he joins me. He stands up on the potty beside me and gives a play by play of my actions. Then...

Captain A: Momma look how much I am. We match tall. Look Momma how big.

[He steps over to the tub and does a complete edition of the cupid shuffle... Singing the entire chorus while dancing on the tub rim. Then resuming our conversation as though there was no musical interlude, he jumps down and stands on the bathroom scale.]

Captain A: Momma... Look how tall! I'm *soooo* much! Momma I'm big now! See? (there's a pause and I feel as though he's looking for mischief) Ummmmmmm... Sometimes Momma... Sometimes, boys need plungers to see how big they are.

Me: Son... I love you. Touch the plunger... I kill you. Get out of the bathroom before you get into trouble.

~~~ ★ ~~~

Parenting Survival Tip # 107: Better get used to the idea of survival of the fittest.

My heart filled a little as my older kids asked if they could watch Finding Nemo. They wanted to watch it in the bedroom... Sitting beside their new fish tank... Because they want to make the fish feel welcome.

Then in walks the Honey Badger. He's chowing down on a loaded bowl of goldfish... Honey Badger don't care.

I realized after about thirty minutes that apparently, Finding Nemo didn't work out. So instead, they settled for the movie Shark Tale. Now are all eating goldfish.

Welcome to our home aquatic creatures! This is what is called "trial by fire". Good luck little one dollar fish! Better get your armor out and your game face on!

~~~ ★ ~~~

Parenting Survival Tip # 108: Teaching them proper dental hygiene is *paramount*!

Captain A marched through the kitchen this morning, and I heard him talking to himself.

"*Ugh*! I hafta hold my breath in so I can't breathe it. It smells *SO* bad!"

Apparently, in the eyes of a boy, asphyxiation is preferable to Colgate.

#ParentingFail
#BrainDamage

~~~ ★ ~~~

Parenting Survival Tip # 109: Listen for the wisdom. It's in there... Somewhere.

Captain A: Oooooooh loooook! Naked sheep!!!
B-Dubya: No. Seriously? Those are goats.
Captain A: No. They're naked sheep.
B-Dubya: (incredulously) They're goats, and they have white hair.
Captain A: Sheep and goats are EXACTLY the same. Sheep just have bigger hair.

#WellPlayedSonWellPlayed
#CheckAndMate
#MasterfullyOrchestrated

~~~ ★ ~~~

Parenting Survival Tip # 110: If you choose to homeschool, brace yourself. You'll be the student. You'll learn *so* much!

Me: Okay. On this page, draw a picture of your best friend. Who is your best friend?

Captain A: My best friend is Justin. (long pause) And turtles. I like turtles.

<div align="center">~~~ ★ ~~~</div>

# Day 16

Promotion is in motion.

*WOOT WOOT!*

Today was the first day of my new hours.

Today was the beginning. No more nights. No more weekends. No more.

Today began yesterday. Well technically... Today began Friday.

I'll explain.

My hubs is coming off his allergy medications. He has a big allergy test on Friday to find out what he's allergic to. I'm thinking it's me. This is an unverified hypothesis.

Let the record state that if we find he's allergic to the kids, I'm rebelling. It's not fair that he may get to bathe in the sun while I sweat if there's a biological reason that he can't handle dirty diapers. The kids make me twitch sometimes too... But he *must* be strong. He *must*!

Friday... He had to go off all allergy medications.

You heard me.

I said... I'll be sleeping in B-Dubya's room until his test. That was the translation. It was the NIV version.

No more meds.

So, Friday was rather normal. Saturday and Sunday passed with little flair.

Yesterday... Oh yesterday.

I went to bed at a decent time. I passed out cold. Open mouth... drooled a tiny bit on my pillow... Whatever... Don't you judge me! I was *exhausted*.

Sleep... Pure... Amazing sleep.

And then the hubs came to bed.

And he fell asleep.

And I was awakened.

I'm not mocking him. In fact, I feel awful for him. There's nothing he can do to help it.

He's done the "Neti Pot" thing. It helps... But there's still some miserableness lying under the surface. Poor thing can't breathe. And I'm *not even about to wake him up*. I'm not going to tell him to flip over. This is night three of him being miserable. He's grumpy. He's tired. Plus, he's waaaaay bigger than me.

If you've ever watched the Discovery channel and seen a sleeping lion, or a grizzly bear, or a crocodile, or a wild frothing mouthed rabid animal... imagine that vivid mental picture.

Now then imagine whatever horrifying beast that is... And picture yourself drawing back your left foot.... and kicking it. Picture yourself without a left foot, ankle and thigh. Only five toes to manicure. No more cute ankle bracelets. No more French manicures. Less to shave... That's the *only* plus.

Exactly... I'm *not* waking him up. I'm *not*. It's not worth it.

Besides, it's not his fault. Just keep my eyes focused on Friday. And do *not* disturb.

He stirs. *Greeeeeaaaaattttttt!*

He asks if I'm okay. I verify that it's difficult to sleep next to an idling chainsaw. I don't say this as much as think it. I mumble incoherently under my breath.

I decide to bail. It's okay. My daughter's bed is comfy.

I stumble across the hall.

I pull her Dora tent off the top of her and throw it in the floor. I neeeeeed sleep, preferably not under a tent indoors.

I curl up.

My daughter has a heat seeking device inside her behind. She's designed like that. If there is a warm body in her bed, she gravitates towards it with her sonar. She then proceeds to kick, punch, snore on and wrap herself around whoever the supplier of heat is.

It's absolutely ridiculous.

I ward her off... Twice.

I fall asleep.

I wake up.

She's breathing on me again.

I push her back across the bed.

I shove her towards the wall.

I fall asleep.

I wake up with her on top of me again. Mouth open. Drool running.

Out loud, since I want the world to be angry with me... I state. *"FOR THE LOVE OF EVERYTHING HOLY B-DUBYA! MOVE OVER!"*

It gets better.

Oh... Yes. She's also a cover thief.

So she's snoring on me, with one foot on my forehead. And she's stealing the covers. I'm convinced she eats them in her sleep. I don't know where they go.

I wake up. She's back on my side of the bed... Again.

And she's digested the covers. I'm freezing. It's after 3 am. I'm now officially grumpy.

I go to snatch the covers. She sits up and looks at me. My hand slips off the blanket.

And I... mother of the year... tired amazing Mom #1... punched my daughter in the face.

It was a total accident.

I gasped.

I waited for her to scream.

She didn't.

She wrinkled up her forehead. She glared at me in the dark. Now she's mad too. She just got punched in the face.

She shouldn't have been cover hogging I rationalize.

She doesn't scream. She doesn't cry. Her brow is furrowed. She looks *exactly* like my mirror in the dark. *Unhappy is the best description*. She states clearly.

"Mom. You go sleep on the couch."

I told her to be quiet.

I acted disgruntled... while feeling guilty. I felt like a horrible person.

I tucked her back in and hoped she'd forget that I punched her in the face.

My alarm went off this morning. My daughter's foot was over on the window sill and her head was in the bathroom... and she was covering every square inch of the bed. It's a talent she has. She does 360's in her sleep. As she swallows the covers.

My alarm went off. I said bad things about life and liberty and the pursuit of the American dream under my breath.

I reminded myself how thankful I am for this new promotion.

I stumbled into the kitchen to make coffee.

I snuck back in to make sure I didn't give my baby a fat lip.

I kissed my sleeping snoring husband good-bye.

Friday... Friday... the day of the allergy test... It can't get here quickly enough.

And I'm prepping to sleep on the couch tonight.

It's only fair.

Wish me luck on this new job.

Today was day #1 down...

And hopefully the family and I will survive it.

~~~ ★ ~~~

Parenting Survival Tip # 111: Be *very* careful what you wish for!

I remember when Captain A potty trained, there were *countless* mornings I would be awakened by the yells from the "throne-room". Cries of, "Mooooooooooooom! I'm dooooone!!!!" The yell would echo through the halls, signaling the time to go in with guns drawn and gas masks properly secured.

I remember thinking those days would *never* end. He would *never* be a trust worthy wiper. I remember vividly how the whole world stopped so suddenly at the sound of little feet running to the bathroom. I remember wishing it would be different with my next child.

Today, I was awakened by the voice of my three-year-old, Honey Badger. He was standing on the step beside my bed. It was early. He was looking me dead in the eye. "I pooped mom."

I thought he was joking. I thought, "No way."

I. Was. Wrong.

Be careful what you wish for. Captain A was ok with temporary immobility to avoid a mess. Captain A was loud, but he didn't mind yelling for a second to have a clean posterior.

Honey. Badger. Does. Not. Care.

He'll jump down from the potty when he's done. He'll come stare at you while you're comatose. Then he might book a cruise. He'll probably go walk the dog. It's possible he'll cook a five-course meal and read a book while eating goldfish crackers. And he'll accomplish all of this, with a naked, unwiped derriere.

This child will accomplish all of these things unapologetically.

Be careful what you wish for!

~~~ ★ ~~~

Parenting Survival Tip # 112: It's alright… In spite of the eccentricities, his friends will still love him.

I handed my son a shirt. He didn't immediately put it on.

Captain A: This is Zeke's shirt.
Me: No, it's not.
Captain A: Yes, it is Mom. I have my karate shirt with my uniform.
Me: You have more than one white shirt.
Captain A: This is Zeke's shirt Mom. It smells like him. I know it's his shirt. I sniffed him while he was sleeping. That shirt smells like Zeke.

~~~ ★ ~~~

Parenting Survival Tip # 113: They set their sights high. Encourage them to aim even higher.

Captain A: Mom, is front flipping being a responsible adult? Because I can do front flips.

Me: It's not exactly being responsible. It's a talent though.

Captain A: Well I have that talent. If I'm not careful... And I don't use it... God could take that talent away from me. I totally use that talent. I can do that all the time. But one time... I kneed myself in the face. I hit myself in the face... With my knee... In my eye. I hit myself in the face with my knee. It was bad. My friend's older brother can back flip. I want to back flip *and* front flip. Like him. And *not* knee myself in the face.

#LifeGoals

~~~ ★ ~~~

Parenting Survival Tip # 114: Always have people on standby in case you end up needing emergency medical services.

Just had the "pleasure" of eating a piece of candy that my children made. It was a cherry starburst squished together with a strawberry starburst and grape nerds... Finished off with a topping of peanut butter.

I had people on standby to make sure that if I ended up in the ER, my husband would know that it was the children's fault... And they did it on purpose.

~~~ ★ ~~~

Parenting Survival Tip # 115: They *almost* know a lot of things.

As I'm cleaning out our blender, I'm joined by the kids.

Captain A: Oooh yeeeaahh! You made milk! I wanna drink that.
Me: No. You can't. It's dishwater son. I made dishwater.
Captain A: It looks like milk. And I want some. Can I have some?
B-Dubya: *You can't drink that!* You'll get hypothermia.

(blink..pause...blink... blink) Yes. This really just happened.

~~~ ★ ~~~

Parenting Survival Tip # 52: Just smile and wave boys, smile and wave.

Got really frustrated when I sat down and realized that the four-year-old hadn't wiped off the toilet seat... Again.

Then I remembered, that wasn't it at all.

*Nooooooooo...* I was jumping to conclusions.

What I remembered... In that part of my head that hides painful memories to minimize the trauma... As he was getting ready to flush and wash his hands... He sneezed.

Even. Better.

#LifeWithBoys
#GonnaBeTheDeathOfMe

~~~ ★ ~~~

Parenting Survival Tip # 116: They'll stake claim to things you'd never imagine. Let them.

I just heard the opening bars to a Disney movie in the back bedroom. I recognized the first few notes that play at the very beginning when the castle and fireworks display on the screen. As the melody played, I heard Honey Badger scream...."*Ooohhhh This is my song! IT'S PLAYING MY SOOONG!*"

Such a passionate lil' fella.

~~~ ★ ~~~

Parenting Survival Tip # 117: If you take their honesty personally, it will one day destroy you.

Captain A: That's the letter "m".
Me: What words sound like mmmmmmm?
Captain A: Mommy says M!
Me: Good job! And what else says M? What does a cow say?
Captain A: Mooooooooooooo.
Me: Yes! So review. What's a word that starts with "m"?
Captain A: Uummmmmmm... I don't know.

Me: You can do this son! What starts with an "m"... (Gently
    encouraging... I point to myself)
Captain A: (confidently) Moooooooooo!

[slams book and throws it through the television]

#HomeSchoolingFail
#ThereGoesMySelfConfidence
#NoMorePhonics
#HopeYouEnjoyIlliteracy
#StinkingHonesty
#NeedAGrouponForTheGym

~~~ ★ ~~~

# Day 17

My husband just abandoned me and went to Lowe's. His Facebook status has something to do with animals eating their young. And my children are angelically playing in the tub.

And I just don't understand.

Well… Perhaps that isn't completely honest. Let me rewind.

Today began early.

The Griz went to the tire shop for his truck.

I was alone, facing the heathens of the wilderness by myself.

But I was armed with pancakes… and oranges… and juice… I came prepared.

We survived. But they have been on "GO" all day.

In a forty-five second span, in my kitchen while I'm prepping supper, I took the time to text myself a few thoughts by B-Dubya.

A forty-five second span. No lie.

"Mom. What if you put me in the oven to cook? I bet I'd taste good. It would be hot in there. And I would be juicy... and I like chicken. It's dark in the oven. And hot. Mom. It's hot in there. It's hot in the oven. Could you cook me? Can I help with supper? Mom. Mom... *Mooooooom*. What if we had carpet over the whole house? Even on our roof? And what it we poured sprinkly sparkly water over the whole house? And we were fairies. Wouldn't that be cool Mom? Wouldn't it Mom? And I want to be fairy. Captain A could be one too. Daddy wouldn't like it. Can I have juice? I haven't had any allllllllll day... Except once. It was orange juice. No, I want milk. Ooooooh! Can it be chocolate milk? I love chocolate milk! I can make it myself instead... Can I? Mommy... Mommy... Mommy."

I zoned out I think. I began looking for household cleaners to sip on. Just pop a straw in. I'll have it on ice so it'll go down smoother, and I'll just go to sleep.

And I handle that energy most days better than my adoring husband. He can't keep up. He tries... But it's a tad overwhelming. In fact, he does an incredible job most days. But today, they were on a different type of level. It was noteworthy.

Two and one half meals cooked. One portrait finished. Two loads of laundry. Vacuuming the house. And all day referee. No joke, I'm ready for bed.

The Griz and I go out on the porch to check on the chicken that's on the grill.

One moment of blissful silence.

The chicken looks great. I turn around to come inside.

And realize in horror... Captain A has locked the door.

He's standing inside. I can see him looking at me. He's saying, "Out. Out Mommy. Door. Broke. Door broke mommy. Out..."

I look over my shoulder. I started fasting and praying. Neither one of us have keys.

B-Dubya is in her bedroom. She's back there playing. She can't hear us.

Captain A gets bored of talking to me. I watch him as he goes over to the table and commandeers his sister's juice. He looks back over his shoulder, apparently wondering why we aren't coming inside stop him. Wondering why we aren't telling him to get his leg off the table. Even his tiny mind realizes that this situation is ridiculous.

Add to this the important fact that we have padlocks on the gates to our fence. And the keys to those padlocks... are on our key rings... In the house...

One of us is going to have to scale the 6-foot chain link fence. If you've ever met me or my husband... you'd know why this might be a problem.

In times of crisis, one has three options that I can think of instantly. Some people resort to tears. They are overwhelmed. They just can't function. Some people grind into gear to accomplish the task at hand. They work best under intense pressure. Some people laugh. It's just a natural response in a hard spot. They see the humor and irony of life.

I grasp option number three. I begin to giggle. I'm not a giggler by nature, but I'm trying to laugh quietly. I look inside at my littlest. He's sitting there in the kitchen with his back to us. He doesn't even realize he's locked us out. He's two. He doesn't understand doors. He's not a bad kid that's being vindictive. He was trying to come out. And he flipped the lock. And now he's looking at mom and dad, and they're playing outside on the porch, and he's miffed that he can't come out.

We bang for B-Dubya.... Nothing.

We bang again.

Nothing.

I. Am. *Dying*. This is seriously funny. But apparently, it's only hysterical to me.

The Griz is furious.

He chooses this moment to break the news that this is the third time this has happened to him at the hands of this particular child. I wasn't aware of the other mishaps.

I can't get it together. I truly can't breathe. The laughter is escaping in puffs now, belting out and my breath is short.

I'm knocking, banging, hoping B-Dubya can hear us because at this point, I'm very close to wetting myself.

Captain A is standing there looking confused.

I look back at my husband. He still isn't seeing the humor. He is very obviously still mad.

I am... useless. I'm weak kneed from laughing and trying to stay under the radar of my husband who looks like he's just licked a nine-volt battery. He's *not* happy.

I get an idea.

"*Captain A!*" I shout. He hears me. He turns to me in slow motion. "*Go get B-Dubya! GO GET YOUR SISTER MAN! GO GET HER!*"

He's standing there. Looking at me. He turns his head. "Sister." He says. "Come here." He doesn't even say it loudly. Just says it. He's looking at me, and talking in a normal voice in my direction. How does anyone survive past the age of two? I'm beginning to doubt that he will. I realize the sheer gravity of our situation. She's never going to hear him. We're going to die outside.

I'm still laughing. I can't even help it.

The Griz is...*not*.

Captain A runs down the hall. Just like that, he's gone, and we're stuck.

Tears are streaming down my cheeks. I look over at my non-laughing husband, and with everything in me I try to pull it together. I finally reign in my hysterics... Mostly.

Straight forward and directly to the point my husband states, "He's going to forget us. He's never coming back."

I lose it again. I'm worthless as a supporter in this situation.

About three minutes later, and after some heavy banging on the door B-Dubya appears.

She saved the day. We get inside at the chicken sizzles on the grill. Daddy announces he's leaving and going to Lowe's, and he's not making any promises as to when he's coming back.

B-Dubya looks at me. "Mommy... Why are you crying?"

And I can't even answer. Tears still streaming, while trying to be cognizant of the fact that I'm a terrible wife at this moment. There's not an ounce of sympathy, only laughter.

Whew! What a day.

Laugh or cry... Today... I choose to laugh... Hysterically.

And I'm getting the kiddos out of the tub to put to bed.

So husband of mine, if you're on your smart phone reading this... On your way to Atlanta... or Florida...

It's safe to come home.

The beasts have been tamed.

~~~ ★ ~~~

Parenting Survival Tip # 68: Cherish your spouse. Without whom, it could have been you.

That moment... When you realize that in your absence... The three-year-old Honey Badger somehow managed to knock over an entire display rack of sledgehammers while shopping at Home Depot with his father. Sledgehammers. Take a moment to let that sink in. The noise... Of an *entire* rack of sledgehammers bouncing off the concrete flooring... In public.

And you immediately realize... Long days are *all* about perspective. Mine wasn't really so bad.

#ThankGodForHubs

~~~ ★ ~~~

Parenting Survival Tip # 119: Yeah. That name works. Not every battle is worth fighting.

Honey Badger: Can I have a cookie?
Me: Those are crackers. Ritz crackers.
Honey Badger: Ok. Can I have a cookie? A cracker cookie?

~~~ ★ ~~~

Parenting Survival Tip # 12: Don't judge. It COULD have been zombies. It really could have.

From the other room...

Captain A: (screams like a girl) *Eeeeeeeeeeeek!!! Aghhhhh.* Don't *ever* do that to me again Honey Badger! Ever! I thought that was a zombie touching me! And you aren't a zombie. Well... You *could* be a zombie. Don't do that!

~~~ ★ ~~~

Parenting Survival Tip # 121: Be careful with the example you set. They see *everything.*

Just watched in horror to see my son's head tilted back... His eyes bulge... Fear cross his face... As a fountain of water spouted out of his mouth... across his tv tray and into the floor. He then coughed... sputtered... and choked until he could breathe again... (During this whole performance, the gears in my head are turning... And realization struck.)

Me: Son... Have you been watching your daddy gargling salt water because he's sick? Have you been taking notes?
Captain A: (non-nonchalantly) Yep Momma. But I'm not sick momma. I shouldn't do that again. I coulda died.
The Griz: It's absolutely *amazing* that *any* little boys survive childhood.

Boys... The *only* reason I'd ever consider taking up drinking heavily again.

~~~ ★ ~~~

Parenting Survival Tip # 122: Don't ask. Just don't.

Captain A: *Awwwwwwww. This* is *EXACTLY* why I didn't want to come to Hobby Lobby on a rainy day!

Me: Why?

Captain A: *Becaaaaaaaaaauuuuse* I just dropped my penny!

#Logic
#YoureDoingItRight

~~~ ★ ~~~

Parenting Survival Tip # 3: Don't ask questions. You really *REALLY* don't want to know.

B-Dubya: Momma, can it be Captain A's chore to wash the front door?

Me: Sure.

Captain A: *Noooooo!*

Me: Yes. He can have that chore, since he's the one who licks the glass.

Captain A: No I don't! That's Honey Badger!

Me: (poking at him) Not since yesterday huh boy?

Captain A: (pausing in contemplation) I licked it yesterday... Because well... I didn't understand the rules then.

~~~ ★ ~~~

Parenting Survival Tip # 27: Yes. You just said that. Don't try to understand why.

The Griz: Son. This is how you get hurt. You're doing dumb stuff. Now go take that chair and blanket off your head, and put them in your room.

~~~ ★ ~~~

Parenting Survival Tip # 52: Just smile and wave boys, smile and wave.

I'm minding my own business, walking through the kitchen. I overhear this conversation.

B-Dubya: (half whispering) Go get a baby wipe. Hurry.

Captain A: I am. Hold on a sec.

B-Dubya: *Hurry.* It's guts are spreading on the table. And they're bright green.

Me: (no... I can't ignore that.) *Seriously?!* Did you kill a bug on my table?

B-Dubya: Possibly. I might have cut its behind off. That didn't work out as planned. The Doctors have done it again. Another bug.... Now in heaven.

#CleanMyTable
#GirlsAreGrossToo
#DoNotTouchMeUntilYouWashYourHands

~~~ ★ ~~~

# Day 18

A memory from May 2011:

When it's Saturday morning...

And you have two small children...

One in diapers and one who is five...

There is very precious little time for snuggling in and sleeping late.

I accepted that a long time ago.

I'm okay with that.

I love to snuggle with them instead. They make life better. I'd take a just one Saturday with my kiddos over a million days to sleep late...any time.

I love the warmth of their pj's and the sound of their sighs.

But...

When one has a five-year-old that has boundless energy and a great imagination...

Saturday mornings are filled with lemons.

Yes, I said it.

Lemons.

On an ironing board. Yes. I said an ironing board, of all things.

The aforementioned ironing board is set up with coupons, and cups, and tissues for use in the event that she sneezes. She's ultra-prepared. She also has a bucket of pennies (pennies that she dug out of the toy box where her brother dumped them yesterday) All of these things added together compose a completely prepared lemonade stand.

And while a completely prepared lemonade stand is wonderful, it's just not the same as snuggles on a Saturday morning.

I look at the clock and it says eight o'somethinghahahaaayou'reawakeinthemorningandyouhaven'thad anycoffeeeeeee....

Yes. My clock mocks me...

My daughter sticks a lemon under my nose and says, "Doesn't that smell like part of a skunk Mom? It's so cool!"

I turn my head to see my son using a pink flute as a telescope while surveying the living room for something to destroy.

Undeniably, Saturdays have taken on a new tone for me. No snuggles. Saturdays are now entrepreneurial.

Verrrrryyyyy interesting...

By the time I'm subjected to the skunk smell, I've already given her all my pennies, which she so generously and promptly returned so that I can buy even more lemonade because, "See what a great deal Mom!?!"

I sigh, knowing a good mother would frequent the ironing board and applaud the lemons and the talents of my eldest.

But I've already had two glasses of lemonade...

And no coffee....

On the down side... the honest side ... I'm tired, and I need an IV of caffeine please and thank you. Also, I'm not a fan of skunk lemons.

But on the flip side... I'm hydrated.

Keep focusing on the positive. You'll survive.

~~~ ★ ~~~

Parenting Survival Tip # 123: Do *not* negotiate! They'll find loopholes!

Honey Badger: Momma, can I have a cookie?
Me: (as I'm rummaging through the fridge) No. You can have some carrots though.

Honey Badger: (peering into the fridge over my shoulder) Ummmmm, Momma... Can I have some vegetables? (pronounced bej-tables)

Me: *Yes!* You can!

Honey Badger: *OH YAY!!!!*

Me: What kind of vegetables do you want?

Honey Badger: Ummmmm... Just vegetables.

Me: What kind? What are vegetables made from?

Honey Badger: (matter-of-factly) They're made out of cookies.

~~~ ★ ~~~

Parenting Survival Tip # 124: Say nothing. Back away slowly.

Honey Badger: I don't like that stuff.

Me: Your ice cream?

Honey Badger: Yes. That stuff has ice cream in it. It has cold. I don't like cold ice cream.

~~~ ★ ~~~

Parenting Survival Tip # 125: You'll get used to the noises of having kids. You really will.

Never mind that sound. It's just the three-year-old...Who crammed 3 carrots in his mouth... At once... Because as soon as he finishes them, he gets a graham cracker.

So now... He's gagging in the kitchen.

#CarryOn

~~~ ★ ~~~

Parenting Survival Tip # 126: You can't prepare for all conversations. Just brace yourself. Always. Brace yourself. Just... Stay braced.

Shy: Do you know how to speak British?
B-Dubya: *Yeeesss!* Bon Jour.
Me: That's French.
B-Dubya: Ne how?
Me: That would be Mandarin.
B-Dubya: Good'aye mate.
Me: Please. You're killing me.
B-Dubya: That's all I've got. I give up.

~~~ ★ ~~~

Parenting Survival Tip # 127: Be prepared for lessons in drama, misinterpretations and overreacting.

B-Dubya: *Ughhh!!* There's baby barf in my sweet corn!
Me: You have almost finished it already. Besides, that's Parmesan cheese.
B-Dubya: *Wheeeewww!* I'm so glad.

[Thirty Minutes Later]

Captain A: *Ahhhh!* Mommy! There's something all over me! It's blood! *It hurts! Owwwwowwwww!*
Me: Or... perhaps...maybe... it's your spaghetti sauce from supper son.

Captain A: Oh! Whew Mommy! That was close.

~~~ ★ ~~~

Parenting Survival Tip # 128. Sometimes, it's good to know exactly what they're talking about.

Captain A just came running into the kitchen. He was soooooo excited! This ALWAYS spells trouble.

Captain A: Mooommaaaaa! (out of breath) I just saw Daddy use that stuff that you put on your boobs!
Me: (blink...blink... blink... blink) What in the world are you talking about???
Captain A: That stuff. You know. You use it every day Momma.
Me: (very concerned because there is *absolutely* nothing in my house that fits that description) Ummmm... Show me son. Please clarify.

We walk to the bathroom and he picks up the hairspray. He shakes his head and sets it down. He then picks up some apple scented lotion. No. Not that either. He shakes his head and puts it down.

Captain A: *Here it is Momma! This stuff!* (he hands me my deodorant) Daddy put this on his arm pets... Just like you!

~~~ ★ ~~~

Parenting Survival Tip # 129: What goes around comes around.

Heard screaming tonight and a flock of little wet cold naked bodies erupting from the bathroom.

Captain A noticed his brother was standing up in the tub. He didn't stop him. Big brother didn't bother to encourage little brother to sit down.

However... When Captain A's shoulder got very warm all of the sudden, he was *immediately* rather offended by his baby brother's choice in where to potty and aim.

#BrotherSkills
#ThatsLove
#PayBackFromWhenYouPoopedInTheTubWithYourSister
#ImGrossedOut

~~~ ★ ~~~

Parenting Survival Tip # 130: Say it. They won't listen. But say it anyhow.

Me: It's kinda warm. Taste your hot chocolate carefully to make sure it doesn't burn you. Blow on it. And sip slowly son.
Captain A: *Ohhhh Mooomma!* I think I just burnt my whooooole lips off. Both of 'em. Do they look gone? Do they momma?

~~~ ★ ~~~

Parenting Survival Tip # 131: Don't ask. And *definitely* don't look back at them while driving. You don't want to know.

Captain A: I just sneezed out a french fry. *Oh! There it is!* Can't waste.

167

~~~ ★ ~~~

Parenting Survival Tip # 132: Relish the fact that at least you're not the only one who struggles.

B-Dubya took the opportunity tonight with a captive audience and read to the boys about Rosa Parks while they were in the tub. At least twice I heard her say, "Captain A... Do you want to hear this story?" Both times he answered in the negative. She told him to shush and kept reading. Honey Badger was singing "What Does the Fox Say?" throughout the entire history lesson. I came in and asked Captain A if he had learned anything, and was he paying attention. "Yes momma." I asked him what she had been teaching. His response? "Red." I stared at him. "You know momma... Little Red Riding Hood." B-Dubya walked out of the bathroom downtrodden. Her history lesson had turned into a big mess.

Me too little girl... Me too. *Every single solitary day of motherhood.*

~~~ ★ ~~~

# Day 19

A memory from April 2011.

My daughter has discovered her voice.

It's operatic...

And I don't even know if that's a word, but if it is...

I'm going to define it.

Operatic: Adverb.   1.   The sound that's currently exuding from a five-year-old.
                        2.   Painful.
                        3.   Currently happening... Without ceasing/stopping/or break.
                        4.   Relentless.
                        5.   Making the dogs uncomfortable.
                        6.   Not musical in nature.
                        7.   Bursting forth with great effort.
                        8.   Noise. Incessant. Painful. Noise.

Yep... That about covers it. Operatic.

She's been doing it for two days now.

Singing answers to questions.

Singing lullabies to her baby.

Singing to her brother to stop jumping on the bed... While he jumps and shouts, "*Stop it B-Dubya!*" He apparently isn't a fan of opera either.

She sings... Endlessly.

I love her. I do. But something has got to give. 'Cause I'm completely played out on the Key of E flat/F sharp/B minor on a Bass scale all at once.

If she were singing on pitch... on key... in some discernable pattern, I could handle it. Make no mistake, even now I encourage her to sing. But I don't completely encourage her to sing exactly like this.

This is... Interesting in nature.

But as her biggest fan, I would never tell her to continue this. I'd tell her to read a book, color a picture of a moose, make lemonade, build a replica of the Eiffel Tower, go on vacation to Disney, learn Latin. Something... ANYTHING but this.

Unfortunately, she can't read yet.

So, I can tell you honestly and without prejudice...

She's killing her mother.

Slowly.

And her mother loves her unconditionally.

Now, the dogs on the other hand... They're a different story entirely. In fact, I caught a hint of their conversation on the back porch tonight as they snarfed down some Kibbles and Bits... and the dogs... they're ready for a revolt.

~~~ ★ ~~~

Parenting Survival Tip # 3: Don't ask questions. You really *REALLY* don't want to know.

B-Dubya: Honey Badger! You shut your fat mouth! I'm not being
　　mean. You have extremely large lips for someone your age!
Honey Badger: (laughing) I don't even have lipstick on my mouth.
Captain A: Honey Badger's lips are like the sign of America. The *flag*!
Honey Badger: *I'm not even wearing lipstick!*

~~~ ★ ~~~

Parenting Survival Tip # 133: The absolute best time to glean insight into their personalities is while driving and listening to back seat conversation.

Captain A: I have toothpicks. They taste like Jurassic World.
B-Dubya: What does Jurassic World taste like?
Captain A: Like dinosaurs.
B-Dubya: How do you know what dinosaurs taste like?
Captain A: Because I've licked one.

B-Dubya: Ewwwww!!!

Captain A: You know, I licked you once.

B-Dubya: I know. You've licked me a lot.

Honey Badger: I lick you too.

#FacePalm

#ParentingFail

~~~ ★ ~~~

Parenting Survival Tip # 68: Cherish your spouse. Without whom, it could have been you.

I just heard rumor that my six-year-old just pooped in the great outdoors.

And he's at his best friend's house.

These people, they *have* a bathroom.

So, he made the *choice* to do that outside.

I'm stating for the record:

#1 That women genetically can't determine male/female traits in children... So this ain't my fault.

#2 I'm not there. So, *this time* when he pooped in public... It wasn't on my watch.

~~~ ★ ~~~

Parenting Survival Tip # 134: Sometimes, just let their imaginations run wild.

In the car on the way home I had a lesson in the life cycle of butterflies.

B-Dubya: (confidently) A caterpillars' life cycle. I know *alllllllll* about that.

Shy: I got a bad grade on this in school, but now I know. They eat the larvae.

B-Dubya: Yes. Me too. They eat the larvae, and then they go into a cocoon. Then they break out of the cocoon and during the hot part of the year, they move to Florida.

Captain A: Yes. That's it. The worms put on their clothes. Then they all go to Florida.

~~~ ★ ~~~

Parenting Survival Tip # 3: Don't ask questions. You really *REALLY* don't want to know.

Me: Captain A, did you wash your toothpaste spit out of the sink?

Captain A: Yes ma'am, I did. And I also got my wedgie out. Now I'm going to say prayers.

Alllllrighty then.

~~~ ★ ~~~

Parenting Survival Tip # 135: There are times when it's socially acceptable to not share.

Is it horrible that I just found two unopened mini Kit Kats in the wash after they'd been through cycle? And since the packages were still slightly puffed... It meant to me that they were indeed still air tight.

So... Without delay... I ate them.

~~~ ★ ~~~

Parenting Survival Tip # 136: Leave the room quickly. And shut the door. You're not a bad parent. They *never* stop talking. Ever.

Okay... Your back is now lotioned... But not with "girl" lotion. You've had a drink. You both have teddy bears... Your brother is asleep... Stop talking... I love you too. No, we're not going swimming tomorrow. No, we're not leaving for Georgia tomorrow. No, I'm not getting on to her for telling you what to do. You *do* need to hush. It's late. I love you too. I'll check into the Old West museum. I'm not making any promises. No, I'm not finding a pillow for your teddy bear. He'll be fine. I don't care. I'm not supposed to be fair. I'm a mom. I love you too. Don't come visit me. It's bedtime. Good night.

~~~ ★ ~~~

Parenting Survival Tip # 137: Cutting corners is sometimes acceptable.

We ushered sleeping kids out of the hotel at 7 AM to get daddy to class on time. No teeth brushing... No morning juice. Just sleepy kids. Sleepy mommy. Captain A unbuckles in the parking lot and leans over my shoulder.

Me: I'm thankful for gum today. Your breath smells good son, even this early in the morning.

Captain A: (exhaling through his nostrils gently on my cheek) So mom... How does my nose breath smell?

Me: Good son. It's all good.

~~~ ★ ~~~

# Day 20

A memory from August 2011:

> *No babies were harmed during the making of this life*
> *lesson. During this time, he managed to actually pee in the*
> *potty twice. Not through his own efforts... He just forgot*
> *that this is what I wanted and accidently did it.*

Book in hand...
Baby boy on potty...
Lesson Time... I'm feelin' froggy.

Me: Captain A ... Are you a baby?
Captain A: Ummmm... No.
Me: Captain A? Are you a big boy?
Captain A: Yes.
Me: Captain A. Look at me. Look at me... *Look at me!*
Captain A: O-tay.
Me: Only babies pee in diapers. Do you understand?
Captain A: Truck.

[What in the world? Ugh. I can't. I'm losing ground]

Me: Captain A, Pay attention. Captain A. Are you a baby?
Captain A: No. I a big boy.

Me: Good job! You're a big boy. Now...Captain A. Look at me. Look at me. *Look at me.* Captain A... Where do big boys go potty?

Captain A: Captain A.

[Yes. He answered that question by saying his name. I'm thinking of dunking my head in the potty and flushing. This is extremely frustrating.]

Me: Captain A. You're a big boy. Big boys use the potty.

Captain A: Yes.

Me: So you need to pee in the potty... And not in your pull-up. Captain A... Where do you go potty?

Captain A: In potty.

[*Yaaaaaaaaayyyyy!* I'm getting somewhere.]

Me: Captain A. Where do you go potty?

[I'm thinkin'... He got it right once... Now some positive reinforcement.]

Captain A: Firetruck.

[Is this real life? Out of left field... I lost all my imaginary ground I just made.]

Me: (speaking out loud to my toddler, as though he understands) I'm a terrible mother... and I'm useless. I don't know how you'll ever get a college football scholarship if you think firetrucks have something to do with potty training. If you don't catch on to this simple lesson son, you're going to grow up without having any friends. I'm concerned for you and the possibility that you aren't going to contribute anything to society.

Captain A: (blinking and staring)

Captain A: No. I a big boy.

Me: Potty. Tell me when you need to go potty. So you can be a big boy.

Captain A: I a *big boy*! (Now he's getting frustrated... But I got dibs on the whole "stick your head in and flush thing"... I thought of it first... and we both have humongous craniums... We won't both fit... If he wants to rid himself of this misery... He's gonna have to find another throne to dunk his head in.)

Me: Captain A. Just tell me when you need to potty. Just tell mommy. Be a big boy.

Captain A: I judo chop you. Judo... CHOP.

[And then he did. He judo chopped me... While he was sitting on the potty. This child judo chopped me, with a pink princess pull-up around his ankles. He judo chopped me. Oh... Don't you dare judge me! They were leftovers from B-Dubya's potty training days... And pull-ups are expensive, and I'm NOT apologizing! He's just peeing on them anyhow... Because he thinks potty time correlates with firetrucks]

Me: Son, I give up. You're not a baby. You're a big boy. Big boys use the potty. Do you understand?

Captain A: I want my daddy.

Me: Your daddy doesn't pee on himself... Try to emulate him.

Captain A: (blinking and blankly staring)

Me: Captain A... Do you think I'm a failure?

Captain A: Firetruck.

I quit. I surrender. Tomorrow is fresh and new... And as he toddles down the hall with his little cheeks jiggling...His pink pull up in the trash... and his mother sitting dazed on the side of the bathtub contemplating dunking myself... I say a silent prayer that my son's friends are forgiving when he grows up... Because he's gonna need that grace.

~~~ ★ ~~~

Parenting Survival Tip # 138: Remember that they get offended by the little things.

Honey Badger walks in... Very distressed.

Honey Badger: I keep trying to play my game. And Wanda is loud. She's in the kitchen. And she keeps banging that thing.
Me: Play your game and ignore Wanda. She isn't hurting you.
Honey Badger: But she keeps banging that thing. It's loud.
Me: Her tail?
Honey Badger: Yes. That thing.
Me: She loves you. She's happy to see you. Go tell her good morning.
Honey Badger: Oh. Okay.

And he walks out.

~~~ ★ ~~~

Parenting Survival Tip # 139: Teeth brushing is *not* optional... and that has *nothing* to do with cavities.

Four-year-old awake. Commence not breathing while he's talking until teeth are brushed. Just felt half of my face melt off.

#DragonBreath

~~~ ★ ~~~

Parenting Survival Tip # 140: Hand out the awards. *Hand them out!*

"I'm sharpening my finger," He announces. "Uuuugghhhhh! *Owwwwwww!"* He yells as he pulls his index finger from the sharpener hole in the back of the crayon box.

I never thought to warn him about that. I over assume sometimes that my kids have any sense at all. I need to start making random warnings. "Son, *you're* the reason my hairdryer says not to shower and blow dry."

Darwin is ALIVE and well in our house... I'm going to start handing out the awards soon.

~~~ ★ ~~~

Parenting Survival Tip # 30: Sometimes, they won't need correction. Sometimes, they're right

Captain A: *Moooom*...Tell sister I'm *not Mexican*!
B-Dubya: (unapologetically) Well, tell Captain A that I'm not Italian. Ummmm… Momma....What are we?

Me: (smiling) You're bi-racial. (They look at me quizzically, so I explain.) It means you're white mixed with African American, and you're all beautiful.

Captain A keeps looking down quizzically at his arm, then to his sister, then to Honey Badger, back to his arm, then B-Dubya... I *know* something good is coming. I can *feel it.*

Captain A: (after a healthy long pause he speaks) Ummmmm. Well... We aren't both bi-racial. Because ... I mean... we don't have the same balance... I mean, *really* mom... I can stand on my head and dance. B-Dubya can't do that.

~~~ ★ ~~~

Parenting Survival Tip # 141: Being a parent turns you into a ninja.

That moment... when you break health rules... get into the kitchen... and out of the kitchen... while surrounded by four children... two of whom are breathing on opposing elbows... one of whom is standing on a stool *directly* behind your left thigh... and you manage to palm three Samoa Girl Scout cookies... place the rest of the package in an innocent looking Ziploc... trash the box... and none of the kids notice.

#LikeABoss

~~~ ★ ~~~

Parenting Survival Tip # 142. It's not sadistic, it's real life preparation.

That moment... After *months*... Of my daughter, *begging* and *begging* and *BEGGING* to eat a can of sardines... and Holly joining in on the begging... Because they *neeeeeeeeeddddd* a can of sardines...

I made the statement, "If you open them... You *will* eat them... The *whole* can. Make a choice."

Nope... They *neeeeeeeeddddd* them.

And now the smells are wafting through the house. And I'm fairly certain that B-Dubya just realized that those fish still have their heads on.

And I said, "If you barf, you clean that up too." And I walked away.

#EpicParenting
#NowTheFunBegins
#LikeABoss

~~~ ★ ~~~

# Day 21

Pffftttttttttttfffffftttttt......

Pffftttttttttttfffffftttttt...

Pffftttttttttttffffftttttttfffffftttttt....

What *is* that? It sounds like a leaking pipe... A moth stuck in a muffler.

Pffftttttttttttfffffftttttt....

Where is that coming from???

Pffftttttttttttfffffftttttt....

Okay... I'm not at all thrilled by this sound. I'm investigating.

We'll get back to that.

To all of you who have ridiculous fears... I understand.

To all of you who can't explain why certain things just don't mix well with your genetics... I get it...

I really do.

It's been raining here. And every time the rain subsides in Georgia... It happens. Slowly but surely... If the temperature is anywhere near comfortable outside... The peaceful humidity settles into the air like a warm wet blanket... and it happens...

The slugs...

Ugh...

The slugs.

I can't handle it.

They aren't nearly as bad at this house as our last. Only a few here and there on the sidewalk. But it's a few here and there too many.

They make me gag. They literally turn my stomach. I can't explain. I've never been bitten by a slug or a snail. I've never been chased to my car by one. I've never worried that I would get a sting that would make my breathing stop.

But I *have* had one stick to the bottom of my sock and roll onto the hardwood floor. And then, I felt it as I slid on the floor after stepping on it... Ugh...I'm going to be sick.

I can't stand them. I would rather deal with a mouse... a feral cat... the measles and a gunshot wound to my thigh... Than to deal with a slug.

So today... The rain has passed. And as surely as a frog bumps its bottom when it hops, the slugs are out. I walked quickly from my car to the house, house to the car. I was watching carefully where I stepped so as not to slip and slide on one of the monstrosities.

I made it safely to and from the school where I collected my daughter. I then quickly made it into the door and locked it. I had zero run ins... No need for a gun. No slippage... WHEW!

I look down on my floor....

And the *horror!*

One of those fiends has found its way into my home, my haven, my fortress. It's freeloaded a ride in on someone's shoe.

I gag. My hands are shaking. This is so stupid. I mean, I can't. I'm shutting down. I can feel my organs packing up shop. They're going to find another body to reside it. I'm about to experience total organ failure. I can't.

I then promptly do what any self-respecting parent would do. I bribe one of the children to fight the demon. I'm shameless. I'm not totally horrid. I mean, I took the time to thank the child profusely... offer snacks and undying gratitude.

I then go to the kitchen to find *The Salt*. Cue the sinister music. I mean *business!*

I take my children outside to learn one of life's many lessons.

It's *essential*... *mandatory*... dare I say even *GODLY* in Georgia... to know how to salt a slug.

I teach them the basics. SALTING 101. Dump and run. Dump and run. Don't stand there for the foaming. That's sadistic. Just dump and run.

They're thrilled! Off they go, searching the highways and byways. I pour into their hands... They dump. It's a team effort. There is enough salt to cover Nebraska roads in December on my driveway. I understand that it's wasteful. I'm good with that. I justify it. I'll cook without salt for a year if it means no slugs.

Slugs are dropping like flies. And there are at *least* two snails that never saw it coming. Captain A got them. Buried beneath a mound of Morton's. Nothing left showing for but the top of the shell. *Take that* you vicious beasts... *TAKE THAT!*

So, we salt the entire county. And surrounding counties too. There's no such thing as too much salt. We then come inside to return to life as usual.

Things are blissful...

Things are almost ethereally quiet.

Then I hear it...

Pffffttttttffffttttt...

I start my search.

Pffffftttffffffttttttt...

I find Captain A standing by the door, bent over, spitting and raspberrying onto my welcome mat.

Me: Captain A... What are you doing?
Captain A: Pffftttffffffttttt....
Me: Captain A... why are you spitting on my floor? Seriously...
   What in the world are you doing?
Captain A: Pffffffftttffffftttttt....
Me: Go outside... Quit spitting on my *floor*!!!! What in the world?
Captain A: *PFFFTTTFFFFFFTTTTTT*.....

And this happens over the course of the next five minutes... Spitting... Gagging... The toddler writhing in the yard. He then dramatically doubles over on his face in the grass...

Captain A: Pffffttttttfffffffttttt!!!!
Me: A... Captain A.... Captain A!!!
Captain A: Pffftttttttffffffttttt....

He stares down at his hand... The same hand I had previously been pouring salt into to dissolve slugs...

Captain A: Pffftttttttffffffttttt.....
Me: Captain A... Son... Please tell me you didn't pick up a slug
   did you???? I'm *horrified* at the thought.

He shakes his head no and continues to spit...

Captain A: Pffffffttttffffffttttttt...

Me: Captain A... Son... Did you taste the salt in your hand?

Captain A: *PPPPPPPPPFFFFFFFFFFFFFFFTTTTTTTTTTFFFF FFFFFFFFFFTTTTTTTTTTT...*

A quick head nod... I'm pretty sure he barfed a little in the grass.

Me: Son... It's just salt... You gonna be okay? You need some water dear?

Another nod...

Captain A: Pfffftttttttttfffffffffftttttttt....

Then he hits me with his thoughts. And with his thoughts, I'll leave you. Remember that I said that it's a blessing to have children. Oh, they make me insane. They make me cry in frustration, but they also make me laugh. He never touched a slug... Only the salt... He kept a good distance. I taught him the art of hunting well... But he was extremely concerned and just needed some reassurance.

Captain A: Mom!!! Check my tongue... I think I have slug germs on it. Am I going to die now?

~~~ ★ ~~~

Parenting Survival Tip # 143: Walk away slowly.

Captain A: It's not black momma. It's *dark* black. And then there's light black.

B-Dubya: There's no such thing as dark black. It's just black.

Me: Son... Light black is grey. Look... Like that car right there. It's grey. There's no such thing as light black.

Captain A: (exasperated and speaking *sloooowly* because I *obviously* know nothing) Mom. That's silver. And our car is white... Also known as *veeeerryyy* light black.

#IGiveUp

~~~ ★ ~~~

Parenting Survival Tip # 144: He'll protect you... He loves you.

I put Captain A on the potty tonight, like we do every night so that he doesn't have an accident in the night. As I lifted him up, he started the weirdest conversation.

Captain A: Ummmm.... The house is in danger.
Me: The house?
Captain A: Yeah. From the bees.
Me: What?
Captain A: The bees. Their light fell off.
Me: Huh?
Captain A: The light. The one... that was on the wheel.
Me: *Okaaaaaaay* son. Let's go back to bed.

I take him back down the hall and give him his Tigger, and I tuck him in. He opens his big brown eyes dreamily and looks directly at me.

Captain A: Momma... I would never let a bad guy do that to the house. *Never.*

Me: You're *such* a good son.

He smiles... and curls up... and he's back asleep.

~~~ ★ ~~~

Parenting Survival Tip # 30: Sometimes, they won't need correction. Sometimes, they're right.

I'm watching an in-depth documentary on homelessness with my kiddos.

Captain A: That's what we do. We hitchhike everywhere.
B-Dubya: No... We don't.
Captain A: Um. Yes, I do. I ride with my Grandpa. So, that counts me as a hitchhiker.

Well played four-year-old... Well played.

~~~ ★ ~~~

Parenting Survival Tip #145: Once they learn to read, life presents a new set of problems.

We were standing in convenience store, when my daughter realized one of life's mind boggling questions.

Me: What's wrong dear?
B-Dubya: I was standing in the store... Reading... I was just reading. And... Ummm. There were these pills there... And they... Ummmmm.... They were for guys.... And I guess I

looked as disgusted as I felt. And the store guy covered them up. So I couldn't see... And I'm glad.

Me: (facepalm and awaiting questions)

B-Dubya: Who would buy those???? (dramatic pause) *And who would get them at a gas station?*

#It'sTooEarly
#NotEnoughCoffeeOnThePlanet
#SoThankfulSheCanRead
#AndMySonsCannot

~~~ ★ ~~~

Parenting Survival Tip # 146: Coffee is a way of life. Embrace it.

Upon awakening, I search for coffee. While I'm in the kitchen, I hear Honey Badger awaken and begin to express his displeasure of the aroma in his bedroom. He announced disgustedly, "Ughhhhhh! It smells like rock wallers and pigs in here!!!"

Not Rottweilers... Rock wallers...

#PourMeTwoCups
#AndNowMyDayBegins

~~~ ★ ~~~

Parenting Survival Tip # 147: Visiting a farm can cause parental aneurysm.

The Griz: (horrified to realize his six-year-old son had just returned after attempting to *catch* a donkey) Son, do you realize that donkeys bite and kick? Really hard! And that could have hurt you badly.

Captain A: It could have bucked me with its forehead!

Granna: Or turned around and kicked you. And smashed your head.

The Griz: (sighing deeply) Don't do that again son. Stay away from the donkey.

Uncle Brian: (coming around the corner of the house) Well... Honey Badger just stepped in afterbirth.

Honey Badger: There was this puddle. Why did I step in that puddle?

Uncle Brian: I have no idea why you stepped in that.

Honey Badger: That was a gross puddle. I stepped in a gross puddle. *Why did I step in that puddle?*

#FacePalm
#NormalDayInFarmLife
#ThanksMom

~~~ ★ ~~~

# Day 22

A memory from March 2013:

I had a new mom ask me a question tonight, and it was one that I could actually answer with absolute certainty. So, I did.

As I was getting off of the phone with her, I thought about her newest addition. The child is amazingly beautiful. That reflection took me down memory lane to *alllllll* the questions I had as a new mother. I was so thankful for all the mothers in my life who answered questions I had about everything when my oldest one was so tiny.

My friend on the other end of the line made the statement to me that I had this whole "mother thing figured out." Honestly... when I got off the phone, I laughed out loud at that notion.

I can be transparent and tell you that I'm stealing a moment to write this in between three loads of laundry and dishes that have *just* been completed... and it's currently 10:28 PM.

Also at the moment, my house is filled to the brim with the melodic tunes of a nine-month-old... who wants to be held... and *not* held all at the same time. He who is desperately tired and *will not* go to sleep. So, he's taking a moment for himself in his crib.

And he's *extremely* offended that I'm not tending to his every need at this... and every single solitary moment of the day.

I enjoy his company so much that I have created a monster, blue eyed, fuzzy headed monster, who doesn't care that there are four other people in this house to tend to. I hope he's contemplating the error of his ways during this moment he's taking for himself.

Now to this new mother, my friend with the amazingly precious baby girl, who thinks I have it "all together as a mom," I need you to listen closely as I share a story... A story of my day.

It actually starts last night... at 10:43 PM... when I realize that the three-year-old that I tucked in at 7:55 PM is still awake.

He doesn't have a night light. I don't have a television on for noise anywhere in the house. His sister is silent. And the baby isn't disturbing the peace.

He's just that tenacious. He has been silently playing... Doing flips... and building empires... and launching rockets.... Silent for nearly two hours.... in the pitch black.

I'm *frustrated*. I'm stunned. I'm tired.

I handle the situation.

He *finally* drifts off to sleep.

Cue today...

The same three-year-old gets up before my alarm goes off.

He's grumpy. He's irritable. He's demanding, and mad because *somehow...* It's *my* fault that he didn't get a good night's sleep.

Whatever. I'm not bitter.

I digress.

I have errands to run, and his attitude improves throughout the day, so off we go.

He's really being quite good, for not having slept and being three. As a mother, I'm impressed.

I'm especially impressed since I've seen his credentials, and his background check, and I know him.

So, as we finish up at the art supply store, I hear him ask politely if he may get a sucker. He asked for one for himself *and* one for his sister.

It was sweet. I'm so proud of the little guy. I acquiesce.

He picks a green one for himself, and a pink one for his sister. He's such a good little brother today.

I'm feeling like a good parent. I've taught him something of value!

I'm in line behind two elderly women with seven-hundred flowers they're buying ... Individually. And it seems that they're counting pennies for each transaction.

My little man waits patiently. He doesn't complain.

I'm *beaming!*

We pay. We get to the car. He buckles in. I open his sucker.

And my day... Oh... my day...

We have one more stop to go. It's ALDI. Yay for fresh produce on sale! Everything in the store is easy to find, quick and to the point. As a busy, distracted parent, I love it!

Halfway through the store, my day begins its downward spiral. Halfway through the store, my halo loses its shine. Halfway through the store, my demise unwittingly begins. Halfway through the store, I see a green streak go flying.

I look at my son... He's very noticeably horrified.

That green streak of movement I saw in my peripheral, that was his sucker.

And it was a *total* accident.

I grab it before he can, scooping it up to toss and keep out of his mouth. He doesn't have discernment in the area of germs and bacteria. I try to be a decent parent and offer him some not so comforting life advice, "Charge that one to the game son. It's gone. I'm so sorry... But you're *not* eating it off the grocery store floor."

I'm attempting to be a good mother. I would never let my child do anything *that* unsanitary... On purpose.

He's understandably upset, but he doesn't complain.

I'm impressed.

I set the sticky sucker in the bottom of the cart, making sure it's positioned in the exact center. I couldn't find a trash can, and didn't want it where he could reach it.

We check out. We get to the car. He never mentions the sucker.

I'm absolutely shocked.

I load up the groceries, and load up the boys.

I look down... We're in the parking lot, and standing beside the car. There is no convenient garbage can, and I need to take the cart back.

No worries... I decided to set it on the bumper of the car. That way, I could grab it off and throw it away in a second... *done.*

I take the cart back.

I get distracted by my son... Who I've just discovered is sucking on a dime. Not just *any* dime. NO! It's one that he picked up off the floor of the grocery store while we waited in the checkout line.

*WHHHHATTTTT???*

I lost my cool for a moment. I made him spit it out. I'm contemplating throttling him and simultaneously dreading his slow languishing demise due to tuberculosis that he just caught from the dime off the floor. I shoved the slimy thing into my pocket muttering under my breath as I remember my mother doing when we were younger... I pondered why I just didn't give him the stupid sucker in the store after it hit the floor. The child is *determined* to catch the bubonic plague *despite* my efforts to be a semi-decent parent.

I drive home.

Captain A never mentions the sucker. My mind is wandering, and I'm still somewhat perturbed by the fact that my son probably just ingested Ebola off of a dime from the floor in ALDI. Lost in deep thought, I'm quiet.

We get sister from school after sitting in a brutally long carpool line. We all evacuate the car upon arriving home.

I go to unload groceries. I come around the back of the car to lift the gate, and I freeze in my tracks. There on the bumper, is that sucker... that stupid green sucker... That stupid pesky emerald blob of sugar and hoof and mouth disease.

As I open the hatch of the car, the sucker hits the ground. I see Captain A is marching around the back of the car to help Momma with groceries. So, I made a decision. I do what any decent mother would do given the circumstances.

To keep my child from the distress of arguing over whether or not he can have the sucker, I hike one foot all the way back and knock that stupid thing under the car. My thought is that later, I'll come back for it. I'm tired, and I don't have the energy to explain my thoughts on bacteria to a three-year-old.

I give him the bread. He carries it in. I know he carried it in. I *know* he did it without stopping. I saw him. I watched him.

I carry the rest of the groceries, and the baby, into the house.

I'm unloading groceries, separating, placing, rearranging, organizing as I go. B-Dubya is at the table tackling her homework. The baby is playing quietly.

The stress of the day is falling off. The kids are content. I have supper on the stove. I have laundry started. I'm in my groove.

At that exact moment, the very moment I breathe in relief over a day completed successfully, I hear B-Dubya say... and I quote... *"OH YAY! CAN I HAVE ONE???"*

And Captain A quickly responds, "Oh yes... I bought you one today too."

And my heart stops as I suck in a deep breath.

*TOO?!* This wording indicates to me... that he *has* something currently in his possession that his sister sees... and wants.

I turn around slowly, knowing, reminding myself to breathe, dreading what I knew I would find.

I saw exactly what I prayed I wouldn't, a flash of green... and a happy boy.

He smiled up at me. He was genuinely beaming.

"Mom look what I found outside!" With that, he pops it out of his mouth and continues. "Don't worry mom... I washed it off in the bathroom."

And as I'm standing in the kitchen gape mouthed and astounded, the child marches off into the living to play with his trucks.

All I can do... is go back to cooking supper. And I whisper a prayer... that whatever super-bug he just purposely ingested... isn't contagious. At the very least, the rest of the members of this household don't deserve to catch whatever it is he wants to grow in his digestive tract. We aren't that gross... We didn't sign up for that.

Please Lord... Let it not be contagious... Amen.

So in closing… To you ... new mother... Sweet friend who assumes that I have my ducks in a row and that my children are angelic… Bottoms up on the heaping dose of reality. Drink it in deeply and enjoy the lingering taste. You're a momma now. You're going to need it.

~~~ ★ ~~~

Parenting Survival Tip # 3: Don't ask questions. You really *REALLY* don't want to know.

I hear Captain A talking in his sleep. This *normally* indicates his little body's need to go potty in the wee hours of morning. So I go in to pick him up. He's sitting up in the bed, staring at, and talking to ... a sleeping B-Dubya. She's *oblivious* to his ranting. I pick him up. I walk him to the bathroom.

Me: (whispering) Captain A. Honey, what were you talking to sister about?

Captain A: (boldly... with his eyes still closed) I need a new gun.

Me: Honey, were you talking to sister about a gun?

Captain A: (eyes still closed) Uhhh... Yep.

Me: What did sister say when you asked her for a new gun?

Captain A: Nothing. She didn't answer. She was at a birthday party.

*Hahahahahaaaaa!* I didn't drill him for any more answers. I figured my baby just needed to sleep that one off.

~~~ ★ ~~~

Parenting Survival Tip # 52: Just smile and wave boys, smile and wave.

No lie. B-Dubya just dragged Captain A down the hall. This was at his own request. Now, please see the visual in your mind's eye. The boy's shorts were down around his ankles. Aaaaand stuck in his shorts... trailing behind him down the hall... is... his bicycle. The whole blessed bicycle. He evidently needed my *immediate* assistance. And I'm of the opinion that taking his shorts off would *apparently* make too much sense. The only drawback was that I didn't have time to take a photo.

#PhotoOpFail

~~~ ★ ~~~

Parenting Survival Tip # 87: It doesn't make sense, but it does make for good stories.

B-Dubya: Me and Captain A were just cleaning out in the yard. We moved the trash can, and we swept the walkway, and we picked the spider lilies.

Captain A: (proudly) And I just cut open a worm in half.

Me: (slow blinks as recognition hits) Ummmm, son?

Captain A: Yes ma'am.

Me: Did you use my dust pan to cut the worm?

Captain A: Yep. But mom, don't worry. He didn't eat the dustpan. He's dead.

~~~ ★ ~~~

Parenting Survival Tip # 148: It wasn't as bad as it could have been. It's not *ever* as bad as it could have been.

Me: (sarcastically) Thank you son. Thank you *sooo* much for sneezing on me.

Captain A: I did not!

Me: You *sooooo* did. It hit my arm. You're gross.

Captain A: (offended) I didn't Momma. Well... I mean I did... But it was only out of one nose side.

Makes *alllllll* the difference. Totally just changed things. It's not gross if it's just from *one* side.

~~~ ★ ~~~

Parenting Survival Tip # 149: The littlest will be taught by the elders. This could be a blessing or a curse.

I hear Captain A getting frustrated. The littlest has zoned in on the fact that big brother has a bowl of cereal, and he's attempting a coup d'état. At the end of his wits, Captain A says *"Here Honey Badger!!!!"*

I look over to see him handing the baby a piece of paper.

Captain A just wants to eat in peace, so he's shoved a piece of home school material at his two-year-old brother. *"Leave me alone and go learn your multiplication tables!"*

~~~ ★ ~~~

Parenting Survival Tip #150: Their imaginations keep life interesting.

While climbing up on the bathroom scale...

Honey Badger: I'm seeing how old I am.
Me: Oh! That's nice. How old are you?
Honey Badger: (looking down at the digital readout) I'm two.
Me: You're three.
Honey Badger: No. I just had a birthday and I got a president.
     And I'm two.

Logic...You're doing it right.

<div align="center">~~~ ★ ~~~</div>

Parenting Survival Tip # 151: If you are resourceful, they will be too.

Totally using a blue corn facial mask to tone just because I can. B-Dubya says all I need is cucumbers to complete "the look."

Sadly, we have no cucumbers.

No worries... Captain A just brought me a jar of mini dill pickles out of the fridge.

#ProblemSolved

<div align="center">~~~ ★ ~~~</div>

Parenting Survival Tip # 152: Little girls need an advocate, someone fighting in their corner. Don't forget how imperative this is.

B-Dubya: If I'm going to be Cinderella... I need a beautiful hot pink dress with no straps.
The Griz: Cinderella's dress was blue.

[blink blink] I have an EPIC husband. He knows what color Cinderella's dress is. Love this man.

The Griz: Just know that when Prince charming shows up at my house... With a glass slipper... I'm heavily armed.

*AND THEY ALL LIVED HAPPILY EVER AFTER.*

~~~ ★ ~~~

Parenting Survival Tip # 153. Enjoy the little moments. They pass too quickly.

The three-year-old just scooted up into the bed beside me. I'm captivated by his big blue eyes, full of mischief, full of life. I just love my children. They're incredible little works of art.

Honey Badger: Morning mommy. The sun is awake.
Me: Yes, it is. Good morning baby boy. How did you get so handsome?
Honey Badger: You cut my hairs. And now I look like daddy. That's what you did.

~~~ ★ ~~~

Parenting Survival Tip # 154: With boys, expect nudity... On a fairly regular basis. In fact, always expect nudity.

I just heard my husband yelling in the front yard where the kids are playing in the sprinkler.

"Son! Keep your shorts on!"

Yep. That just happened. Again.

# Day 23

A memory from January 2013:

I'd like to take this moment to profusely apologize to the couple who was parked beside us today at Zoo Atlanta. We were parked at the top back row of the parking lot, in the white SUV. You had a beautiful sleeping baby in your stroller. This post is written only for you.

*I . AM. SO. SORRY.*

But may I please explain?

At lunch time today, we arrived at the zoo... *finally.* You see, you only have one child. You really have no idea what an act of God it is to get my family fed, pottied, fed again, diapered, dressed, pottied again, and out the door to go *anywhere.*

I digress.

It's warm today... Very warm... May/June warm. Not at *all* January weather. High 70's... Warm. Because we were unaware of the temperature when we got up and got dressed initially, we changed clothes at LEAST 6 times. We *finally* got everyone belted and buckled and into the car. We then drove... forever.

We were *so* excited to be at the zoo. This is the first zoo trip ever trip for any of my children. I haven't been since I was in elementary school. So please understand that we're all very... very... *VERY* excited.

We wedged ourselves between two other parked cars. Thank heavens my husband was driving. But imagine this. Think as thin as is humanly possible. Try not to leave man sized holes where we escaped narrowly from our vehicles. We were *wedged* in. We'd packed a picnic lunch, and we stuffed the stroller down with everything imaginable. We wanted to leave *nothing* to chance.

After we arranged our pack mule, we headed downhill. And that hill... Is *amazingly* downhill. I mean, it's nearly vertical. Thank heavens it's downhill! Easier for us and the stroller which is packed *waaaay* past factory specified capacity. Never you mind! Into the zoo we went!

We got in the door without losing anyone. There were zero bumps... bruises... hurt feelings... or threats being muttered. We're mere minutes into our journey, and I felt like a semi-successful parent.

We got everyone seated at the table. We'd now been there for over two and a half minutes. Record breaking news is that by this point in our journey, no drinks have spilled, everyone's hands had been sanitized, and there was satisfaction on every face. As a momma, I'm feeling like a million dollars.

I took one bite of my sandwich, and as usual, three-year-old Captain A announced he needed to potty.

This is typical three-year-old behavior. We've been here before. I knew we would survive. Off we went. He's big enough to understand pictures now and immediately began to protest. He's *not* a girl, and he doesn't deserve to have to go into the bathroom with the "girl picture" on the door. He's a *boy* Momma! A little *booooyyyy* and this isn't fair.

Got it. I understand that. But since you... oh little boy... have a tendency to dance alone while looking in the mirror... and eat things off the floor... and forget your destination... You shall go with mommy... into the "girl picture" door... and you will do it happily! *Now get movin'!*

Potty done... Check.

Didn't fall in... Check.

Hands washed... Check.

Picked up a step stool while I wasn't looking... sighhhhhs... Check.

Re-washes hands... Check.

Places hands on every single solitary inch of the door that was reachable to a three-year-old while momma is washing her hands for the second time... and then touches the trash can... and the wall... deep sighs from me... Check.

Momma uses bad but justifiable language under her breath and attempts to control her breathing... Check.

Finally get back to the table and just use stinkin' hand sanitizer...
*CHECK!*

I sat back down and swallowed one more bite.

The baby took that moment to begin to wiggle. I looked over at him. He appeared to be digesting his bib. He may have already consumed a burp cloth and his spare shirt. I'm not certain because the stroller was packed so solidly. He's drooling and beginning to work on consuming his own left foot. Note to self... I *do* believe the child is hungry.

I swallowed the rest of my food in one gulp. I'm still hungry, but who cares? I guess I could have eaten my plate and chewed on the remnants of my water bottle. I can't get angry. This was truly a typical meal. Multitasking... This is my life.

I realized that the baby needed to nurse. But that's when it dawned on me that I had no blanket... no burp cloths... and no way to discretely take care of business. In my excitement to be at the zoo, I had packed everything imaginable into the diaper bag to care for B-Dubya... Captain A... and lunch. I had *completely* forgotten the essentials for Sir-Eats-A-Lot.

Now, there were three adults at the table, but I didn't want my mom to have to hike to the car. The other children were still eating, and my husband already appeared tired. So I opted to just go back to the car, take care of the baby, and be about my business.

And this mother of three decided that she didn't need the stroller. *Noooooo...* That would have made too much sense. Nope! Super

Mom was going to just jaunt to the car and do what she needed to do and return quickly.

That was the plan...

In my head...

Stay with me...

Soooo.... I grabbed up Mr-Twenty-Pounds-at-Six-Months-With-Love-Handles-and-Cankles, and I throw him on my hip. I grabbed up the leftovers and empty containers that needed to go back to the car. Off I went.

Unmistakably, here's where things began to fall apart. I got out to the parking lot. Remember the bliss I wrote about while strolling casually downhill into the parking lot? I quietly began to fuss at myself as I realized that Mr-Fluffy-Bottom-Tubby-Thighs and I were going to need rock climbing and rappelling gear to get to our car, which was parked at the *top* of the parking lot. The top row of this aforementioned parking lot which now appeared to be suspended in midair above our heads.

The hike began.

I survived it... Huffing... Puffing... Fussing... Sweating. The baby ate half of my hair and the sleeve of my shirt during this rigorous journey.

I got to my car and took a well-deserved minute... or seven... to catch my breath.

I then looked at both sides of our vehicle. We were crammed between two other unlucky zoo-goers. I hastily decided that there was more room on the driver's side, and that it would be more discrete to nurse a baby in the back seat of the car... simply because it made sense at the time.

In hindsight... I'm very sorry again. *I have no idea why I did that.* In hindsight... I'm sure that at one point in history, bungee jumping appeared to be safe... Butterfly collars were popular... and the Pinto seemed like a sure-fire bet for Ford too... Whatever.

Sooo... I wedged myself into the back seat of the car. I didn't even think about running the A/C. I would only be a minute. Right? So, I locked the doors, took care of the baby, and thanked the heavens that there was no one in the cars parked closest to us to care about my exposition of skin.

I also kept my eyes open for the bored looking security guard who had been casually strolling through the parking lot. I must admit that I had *no* desire to get to know him better... or cause a scene. I'm considerate like that.

I finished what I was doing, and changed the child. Sweat was now pouring from our everything. But no worries, I'm designed to be a survivor like that. And I had *so* much help from Mr-Thank-Heavens-Mom-Didn't-Miss-A-Meal. He was on his way into a blissful milk induced coma. Clean diaper... Happy child.

And then I had a thought.

It dawned on me that I was sitting on Captain A's side of the car...

His door specifically... has child safety locks. And to my horror, I note that they... were... on.

*What in the world am I going to do?*

It was at that moment that I looked to my right. There you two were... A happy young couple casually strolling to your car with your sweet sleeping baby in your stroller. You were both notably in shape. The hike up the cliff hadn't even made you break a sweat. And there sat I... Trapped in the back seat of my SUV with no A/C... slightly sweating and disheveled.

I watched as you scooped your sweet sleeping girl up in your arms and gently placed her in her car seat. She didn't even wake. She seemed to be such a precious angel.

I thought... for one brief moment... about quietly tapping on the window and getting you to open the door for me.

But no... That would have made me look silly.

I couldn't *possibly* have asked a stranger for help.

No... That would have made entirely too much sense.

I decided instead... To do what *any* brilliant and self-assured mother would do. I'd just reach over the seat... slide the keys into the ignition... roll down my window... pop open the door... That way, no one would ever know that I was an idiot and that I somehow managed to lock myself into my own vehicle.

That's how it looked in my head. The plan was fail proof. Scout's honor!

So I slid my baby into his car seat. Step one was a total success. I then reached over the seat. I realized that my precious ever so thoughtful husband had the window lock on. Okay, that threw a little hitch into my plans. "Whatever." I thought. "No worries. I'll just lean a little further and click that button and all will be well."

You... Oh sweet in-shape couple with the sleeping baby... You were then folding up your stroller and quietly talking. You were probably discussing how amazing it was that your daughter was snoozing so soundly while you picked out a destination for lunch. It was probably a destination that served only organic salads and club sodas.

I saw you, but I wasn't really paying attention to you. I took that exact moment to lean precariously, ever so gracefully up front...

I somehow managed to fumble the keys and drop them. *Are you even kidding me right now?* I looked up to see the security guard strolling down our row in the parking lot. But did I even think, "Hallelujah! A salvation from above?" Did I knock on the window and let him know I just need to be let out?

Heavens *noooooo.* Then I might have looked silly. Plus, that would have been *entirely* too much like common sense for me.

I leaned further to grab the keys... It was just a little ways more. But when my fingers finally clamped around those hateful keys, my finger slipped... And I accidentally hit... the panic button.

There was this moment... It's difficult to describe. It was a moment of complete silence... A brief deafening moment of clarity and calm... Before my life ended.

And then... Piercing the silence of your sweet toddler's sleep... The alarms started blaring... Lights started flashing... I think the President was alerted... and the airbags threatened to inflate.

And all the while... I'm was draped over the driver's seat... fumbling with the stupid key... trying *desperately* to shut off the sirens... and un-alert the authorities to the fact that I could have been a robber, *stealing my own blessed vehicle.*

No luck was in the cards for me. My dignity was shredded. My calm, was gone on vacation. But in one final attempt to regain control of my poor life choices, I managed... Somehow... From the back seat... To crank up the vehicle.

I swept my sweaty bangs out of my eyes for long enough to realize that the security guard was staring at me through the windshield. Not helping me. No... Just standing there... Staring.

And you... Oh sweet couple... You billboard couple for REI and Bass Pro Shops, and who probably enjoys long relaxing hikes in the Appalachian Mountains... I'm not sure what you were doing... But I know *for a fact* what I was doing.

I was wedging my wide hind quarters in between the two seats. I stepped into the passenger's seat for a brief moment and then planted my fanny in the driver's seat. I threw my shoes across the windshield, and still couldn't get the blessed alarms to stop going off. It seemed like a lifetime and then...

FINALLY! *SUCCESS!*

Then ... Silence.

I breathed a deep sigh of relief and then noticed that I should probably get my shoe unstuck from the center console.

I brushed my hair off of my forehead.

I noted with a tad of satisfaction that my near-death experience had caused your angel to awaken. Mine was still *wiiiiide* awake in the back seat. He shouldn't be alone in his awakened state.

I adjusted my clothing. And then I did as any self-respecting citizen would do. I opened the driver's side door casually, tripping out of the vehicle and stopping the door just before it hit the Toyota beside us.

I then apologized profusely. It was sincere, heartfelt. You nodded in stunned silence. I'm guessing that you assumed that no competent car thief would *ever* be that clumsy. You looked at each other, quietly got into your vehicle... and I'm *fairly certain* that I heard you double check to make sure all the doors were locked before you backed out beside me.

I collected Mr-Smiles-At-His-Mommy-Even-Though-She-Just-Had-A-Near-Death-Experience from his car seat and acted like nothing had happened. I nodded at the security guard and waved as I strolled nonchalantly by him.

I started my downhill hike into Zoo Atlanta for a wonderful day with my family.

Sweet couple... I'm so sorry your trip ended so poorly.... Hope your little one recovered from her rude awakening... and I hope your organic salad and tofu lunch was tasty.

I hope you'll be happy to know that I only dislocated one joint, and my psychologist says that the emotional scarring from self-induced public humiliation only lasts about six months.

Thank you for not calling the cops on me. My husband just informed me that he would have just walked away from the vehicle and left me stuck inside, and informed authorities that there was a drunk woman trying to steal the car.

Thank you for being better than him... You just locked your doors and drove away... Albeit quickly.

Hope your next trip doesn't coincide with ours... For your sake.

God bless!

Signed ~ One tired momma.

Parenting Survival Tip # 12: Remind yourself often that you're doing the best you can. You're not a failure. It's not you. It's them.

As I'm on the phone I hear Captain A say, "I turned something on for you Momma." With that, he runs out of the room and down the hall.

Netflix is on. I'll admit that am not paying attention. I turn around a few minutes later to see B-Dubya and her friend Maddie focused raptly on the television. They're *engrossed!* There are doctors on the screen, and it appears to be a documentary.

I nonchalantly ask, "So, what are we watching?"

B-Dubya responds, "Weird But True. Mom this show is *incredible!!!* It's about this woman... Who got shot in the chest... and they're putting this bag thing inside of her..."

[blink blink... shake my head... blink blink] Holy cow!!! Those would be implants... [blink blink blink] We're not watching that! *We're not watching that! WE ARE SOOOOO NOT WATCHING THAT!!!*

Thank you Captain A. Now I have to apologize to our visitor's parents.

~~~ ★ ~~~

Parenting Survival Tip # 52: Just smile and wave boys, smile and wave.

Until one has been holding a toddler... and that toddler has sneezed... and a small piece of pulverized french fry has flown up one's nose... One hasn't fully lived...

That is all.

~~~ ★ ~~~

Parenting Survival Tip # 52: Just smile and wave boys, smile and wave.

Never ever let your guard down. They're trying to get you. And regardless what you tell yourself... It's intentional.

Faiiiiirly certain I just witnessed a milk jug being placed in my dryer. This occurred only moments *after* our television remote came precariously close to being eaten by the trash can.

#Toddlerhood
#BringItOn
#ChallengeAccepted

~~~ ★ ~~~

Parenting Survival Tip # 155: Have an emergency stash of 'things to do' in the event of a power outage. Otherwise, you're left at the mercy of the minions.

I've never been so thankful for the return of power to a house! So far, the kids have:

Been ninjas.
Been wolves.

They have shouted.

They have played Legos.

They have been scared of the dark.

They have yelled.

There was a sword fight.

There was running.

There was flipping.

There was shouting.

There was skipping.

There was copious amounts of shouting.

There was talking.

There was yelling.

There was loud and rambunctious shouting.

There was fort building.

They ate apples.

They ate popcorn.

They ate veggie straws.

There was more shouting... Just shouting... And more shouting...
While they were shouting.

And they tormented the dog for what seems like forever. They
call it playing, but I just feel sorry for her. She seems like she
likes it. She's not judgy at all..

But now the power is on, and I can breathe. It's crazy how much
we take for granted.

~~~ ★ ~~~

Parenting Survival Tip # 3: Don't ask questions. You really
*REALLY* don't want to know.

B-Dubya: My lips burn.

Me: Why?

B-Dubya: Because there is bug spray on them.

Me: Why?

B-Dubya: Because I licked my lips.

Me: Why is there bug spray on your lips?!?!?!

B-Dubya: Because I licked my finger.

Me: *WHY?*

B-Dubya: Because there was water on it.

Captain A: (filling in the gaps so that I don't miss part of the story) *Buuuuut* it wasn't water. It was bug spray.

#FacePalm

#IQuit

~~~ ★ ~~~

Parenting Survival Tip # 156: Take the tiny opportunities that life throws you. They're *priceless!*

I was cutting through a tiny block of cheddar cheese. It was a weird angle and every time the knife went through... (*smack*) Onto the cutting board. I was in a hurry. (*smack smack smaaack*) Yay! Sliced cheese! Sandwiches!

From the living room... A tiny voice... A worried six-year-old... "Ummm... Momma.... Are you practicin' your wooden spoon skills for spankins?"

Bwahahahahaaaaaaaaaa!

#IshouldHaveSaidYes
#MaybeI'mStrungALittleTooTight
#FearTheSpoonBoys
#FearTheSpoon

~~~ ★ ~~~

Parenting Survival Tip # 157: Robots are pretty much cooler than *anything* else you could possibly plan.

We had just moved to a new city, and I was looking for things to do.

Me: Sooo. Guys... I just figured out where there's Redbox out here.

Captain A's eyes got as big as saucers. I mean Redbox is exciting... But there's something going on in his head.

Me: Since they have Redbox. Maybe we can rent Turbo the racing snail.
Captain A: (sighs deeply) Ohhhh.... I thought you said there was robots out here. But Redbox is cool too.

~~~ ★ ~~~

Parenting Survival Tip # 158: You *could* mess with their heads... But sometimes that's just mean.

B-Dubya: Those people are from Alaska! Those are from Utah! And those... *whhhhhhoooooaaa*.... (stunned silence) Momma... Their tag says they're from Saturn. (more silence)

Me: Honey, you can close your mouth now... That's the make of the car. They're from Colorado.

B-Dubya: (sighs deeply... dejectedly) I always wanted to meet alien.

~~~ ★ ~~~

# Day 24

A memory from October 2012:

The following is a brief synopsis of the last conversation I had with my children:

I'm helping my daughter with her homework. She's putting words in alphabetical order. STONE - STORE - STOP

"I'm so confused." She gripes. "I don't know because they all start with 'S'."

"I can spell." *Annnnnd* in comes the 3-year-old. Life is about to get more exciting. I can sense it. He's got a basketball in one hand... a half devoured gummy worm in the other.

"B-Dubya," I calmly explain. "If the words match on the first letter, move to the second. And if the second letter matches, then go to the third.

"Ohhhh! I got it!" She announces. She begins to write. Captain A has climbed up into the chair beside her. He's staring at her paper. He then looks at me like I'm an idiot. Of course, he's smarter than me. What was *I* thinking? He's *three* for pity's sake!

"B-Dubya," he says. "That's not right. I can spell. STONE comes first." A long drip of drool runs down his chin and splotches her homework paper. Not just any drool... Half chewed gummy worm drool... That›s gross.

She's disgusted. I can tell. I'm disgusted... and it's not even my paper. "Moooom.... Make him go away. And it's not fair that he knew that. You said the words in order. He cheated."

"*I can spell!*" He re-announces.

"Fine." She says it with such force, I can tell she's prepared to prove him wrong again. I see the gears turning. Her lips turn down at the corners, and she begins to plot. I step back and wait for fireworks. This is *always* the good part.

"You're three Captain A. You don't know everything." She's not being ugly to him. She's only reminding him that he's interrupting her homework, and that he can't tell her what to do. It's a "sister thing" I think.

"Yes." He says matter-of-factly. "I do." He isn't one for ceremony. He's absolutely convinced of his deep and intimate knowledge and wisdom.

"Fine. Captain A.... What is one plus one?" She purses her lips and waits for him to give up. She just knows that she's stumped him.

"Ummmm... One plus one?" He restates thoughtfully. As if repeating the question will make him gain instant knowledge of addition. "One plus one?"

"Yes Captain A. You heard me. You're so smart. Tell me what one plus one is."

"One plus one... Is where you get in your car and go to the store." And with that answer, he climbed down off her chair and took his basketball to go play in the living room.

And now... I'm stumped.

Either the math rules have changed since I went to school... Or I need to sign that kid up for therapy now... He's gonna have some issues later in life.

~~~ ★ ~~~

Parenting Survival Tip # 159: One boy, one brain. Two boys, half a brain. Three boys, no brain. Four or more, we're running a deficit.

That moment... When you hear what sounds to me like a fully-automatic fully high powered rifle in your back yard... Followed by a six-year-old boy screaming, *"Awwesooommme!!!!"* Then you listen as your husband has to go out to speak to your six-year-old and an unnamed five year old and instruct them that it *really* isn't using good judgement to poke sticks into the air conditioning fan.

#ThatJustHappened
#ThankHeavensForHomeOwnersInsurance
#LifeWithBoys

~~~ ★ ~~~

Parenting Survival Tip # 28: Accept reality… There isn't a reason.

Captain A: Wow! Sanitizer burns my eyes. (as though this is a life altering epiphany) I just got it in my eye. I hit the pump *very* hard… Because it was almost gone.

#LifeWithBoys
#BoyLogic

~~~ ★ ~~~

Parenting Survival Tip # 3: Don't ask questions. You really *REALLY* don't want to know.

B-Dubya: Honey Badger! Get out of your nose. That's no place to play!
Captain A: If you were *verrrrry* tiny… You could go up in there and play… And you could spin around…. Until you slipped in snot.

~~~ ★ ~~~

Parenting Survival Tip # 160. Birds and bees conversations… Have them. Don't worry, they'll create the *perfect* opening for these chats.

Me: Wow! What in the world happened to your foot???
B-Dubya: Something bit me today at Granna and Pa's house. It kinda hurts.
Me: Girl, your foot is *soooooo* swollen. Did you see what bit you?
B-Dubya: Ummmmmm… I wonder if it's gonna be a girl or a boy.

Me: What in the world are you talking about???
B-Dubya: Well, look at how swollen my foot is Momma. Isn't it obvious? I'm pregnant.

~~~ ★ ~~~

Parenting Survival Tip # 161: They'll impart all their vast treasure troves of knowledge to whomever will listen. Warn your friends in advance. This will save you from awkward conversations later.

B-Dubya: A rodent is a furry thing. It's like a mouse or a rat or a hamster, and it has a naked tail.
Faith: Oh, like a baby pig.
B-Dubya: Exactly.

~~~ ★ ~~~

Parenting Survival Tip # 52: Just smile and wave boys, smile and wave.

Captain A: Momma. Did you paint Michael Jackson?
Me: Son, no. That's Lena Horn.
Captain A: Oh. (pause) Well... Did she *marry* Michael Jackson?

#FacePalm

~~~ ★ ~~~

Parenting Survival Tip # 162: In certain circumstances, it's totally appropriate to throw one's spouse under the proverbial bus.

While home schooling, I learned that my daughter knows in depth... The process by which pig farmers inseminate pigs. Thank you Mike Rowe with Dirty Jobs... And Daddy.... For falling asleep and not changing the channel. Our lives are *so* much richer because of this.

~~~ ★ ~~~

Parenting Survival Tip # 3: Don't ask questions. You really *REALLY* don't want to know.

B-Dubya: Sick! Are you eating a booger?
Captain A: (matter-of-factly) Nope. Today... They're called croutons.
B-Dubya: You're so disgusting.

~~~ ★ ~~~

# Day 25

A memory from October 2012:

From the back seat of my car I hear it.

"Rrrra... say Rrrraaa...Rrrrraaaaaaaa." It's B-Dubya. And she's gearing up for a spelling lesson. She sounds like a weed eater engine, desperately trying to turn over and blaze to life.

"Aaaaa... Like 'a'... Say it Honey Badger... Say aaaaaa. Short 'a'. Not long. Ra... aaa...." It's a full lesson, including vowel sounds. I giggle quietly.

She's intently looking at her baby brother. Not the three-year-old... Not the one who can actually talk. *Nooooo...* That would be too logical.

No... She's teaching... The infant.

The little one...

With no teeth...

And zero concept of speech.

"Rabbit. Say it, Honey Badger." She's forceful this time, sounding very teacher-like. "Rabbit. Say it. I know you can. Say rabbit."

Honey Badger says nothing. He's a terrible student, I fear. Little ungrateful cuss... Unappreciative of his sister's effort.

She looks disappointed, but nonplussed. She starts again.

"Raa... say rraa... a - a - a - bit. Say it. Rabbit. Rab- Can you spell it?" I'm laughing now, quietly. But I'm shaking in my seat. This is *epic!*

"Come on Honey Badger... You know you can do it!" I don't know what he did at that precise moment, but the words turned to praise. «*Good job* Honey Badger!!! R - A - B." She spells happily. "Yup... then B - A - T... R - A - B - B - A - T."

She notices a discrepancy. "R- A- B- B- A- T. It's spelled dumb Honey Badger. B - A - T spells bat. But you pronounce it rabbit. IT... That's how you say it."

She's *very* stubborn, and today she's *going* to teach him to talk. *Today!* "Say it with me Honey Badger. Rabbit."

I'm up front (dying). I'm laughing quietly to myself. Honey Badger (who is now a whopping four months old, doesn't respond (except to squeak) which is just enough encouragement for her.

Back to the lesson.

"Rabbit... Rrrrrrrrr. Say it Honey Badger... Rrrrrrrrr...."

In jumps Captain A. He's yelling, and I'm not sure why. *"Make him say Spiderman! That's better than rabbit! Rabbits are dumb!*

Now the teacher is offended, but she wants to entertain her other brother too. So, genius child that she is, she comes up with a plan. It's rather smart, if I can give her some credit.

"Captain A," She offers sweetly. "I'll teach him to say Spiderman... If you can spell it. Spell Spiderman Captain A."

Without missing a beat, he replies, "S - Q -R -F - G."

I lose it. Like, I'm completely doubled over. There's no hiding it. Now they both know I'm eavesdropping because they hear me laughing. And perhaps, I kind of...maybe...slightly snorted... just a little. Or a lot... I was laughing. *A lot... L - O - T. LOT.*

And now... my kids are both mad at me. And I'm 100% unapologetic.

~~~ ★ ~~~

Parenting Survival Tip # 3: Don't ask questions. You really *REALLY* don't want to know.

If I needed to eat a worm... At the very least I would need salt ... And probably honey mustard...

~ Random thoughts by Captain A

~~~ ★ ~~~

Parenting Survival Tip # 163: Don't romanticize. Be real.

If you're even *remotely* thinking about the joys of motherhood... and the smells of newborn skin... and *all* the warm fluffies that go with babies.... Please go purchase a cinder block... Place it eye level at a prominent place in your home.... Speak clearly to it... Repeating the same thing seven-hundred-thirty-four times.... Stare at it.... Repeat again... And when it does *nothing*... Then answer whether or not you feel fulfilled.

Welcome to one day of motherhood.

# Day 26

A memory from January 2014:

A List of Animals That Eat Their Young

Rats
Grey squirrels
Ground squirrels
African hunting dogs
Some adult bottle nose dolphins
Butterflies
Gulls
Kangaroos
Cats
Dogs
Rodents

A list. Not comprehensive of course. But a list nonetheless of some animals that eat their young. Fascinating. Horrifying. Utterly unthinkable.

So why am I thinking about it?

Good question.

Here's why.

We ate Chinese today. Buffet style. The whole family. Chinese. Chinese food makes me think of eating my young.

Why?

Again... Great question.

We filled plates. Veggies. Rice. Sesame Chicken. The whole sha-bang. They're well rounded kids.

The vocal one... The four-year-old... He advises me that he'll just stick to broccoli today. "It's green enough mom. That'll do."

I'm swelling with pride. *I love this little guy. Love him.*

We go to sit down and eat.

B-Dubya is veggied and riced up. She's well balanced too. Again... I'm swelling here. Proud momma.

And then...

A young couple comes in and is seated at the booth behind us. I don't even notice. But I see B-Dubya perk up. Whatever. I keep eating, and shoveling french fries to the baby. Happy kid. Happy mom. Daddy is getting refills. I'm alone with the "blessings."

They're whispering. I'm not paying attention. They're eating, and talking, and being relatively calm. So, I'm not really zoned into their conversation.

I should have been.

*I. Should. Have. Been.*

The Captain A is nearing the end of his plate.

As he approaches critical mass, he begins to whisper more to B-Dubya.

I'm oblivious to the fact that the masses... Are getting restless.

I hear him say. "Oh. Let me see that. I gotta see."

And I didn't pay attention.

Parenting fail! *People... I didn't pay attention.*

He stands up on the booth. Turns around... He looks at the other table. The booth next to us. *Right next to us.*

And says... "Yep. He's definitely got a afro." He's still facing the table directly. You know... The table that's *connected* to us by the booth that my four-year-old is standing on. Yeah. He's facing that table. He continues as he turns back to his plate. "Wow. That's a big afro. B-Dubya... He's a clown I think."

He wasn't being ugly. He was kind of in awe. He was admiring the afro. He was stating facts. He wasn't making fun, or purposely demeaning. He was being an observant four-year-old... An observant four-year-old... With no volume button. An observant, loud, four-year-old with no filter and *absolutely* zero concept of public social norms and unacceptable behaviors. A loud observant four-year-old that has no clue in the world that our table... and his mouth... are not protected under a bubble protection shield that silences his thoughts and keep the embarrassment from killing his guardian and keeper.

He sits down.

I shush him.

I re-direct the conversation.

I try not to draw attention to the oblivious little one.

I have to methodically *work* not to climb under the table and fake a sprain, aneurysm, or heart attack to detract from my son's observations.

I take a drink, and listen to their conversation turn. I sigh a big sigh of relief. They have taken the bait. They're now discussing fortune cookies. Whhhhhhhhew... I exhale.

Captain A reaches "full", and I've let my guard down.

*I've let my guard down people!*

He says (as he stands up and stretches, in his no volume tone)

"Mommy. I'm full. I'm *so* full. I don't want any dessert. Can I just sit here and be good and stare at the afro-guy please mom?"

I blink... Twice. As the blood begins to creep up in the veins of my neck into my throat and puddle around my ears and into my eyes and make my nostrils flare slightly.

I say quietly. "Captain A. You can be done. But you need to stop. You're not going to stare at people. It isn't nice. And don't mention him again okay. Please hush."

Again. He isn't being mean. He's in awe. And I don't want to draw attention further to the situation. I want to be cognizant of the fact that he isn't mocking. He's stating facts. We can have a discussion about manners in the car.

He's sitting, opening his fortune cookie. He's thinking. It's been a few minutes. I think we're out of the woods.

He speaks. "Clowns *do* have fuzzy hair." He states. He's not mentioning the stranger at the adjoining booth. He's careful to mind his mom and follow instructions. But I'm following his train of thought. "Clowns' hair is fuzzy. *Very.* Big and fuzzy. And that's clown's job... Fuzzy hair.

He pops a cookie into his mouth and chews. Thinking of clowns and amazing hairdos... And all things four-year-olds contemplate on.

He doesn't speak again of the follically blessed stranger until we exit the building. Instead he's quiet, thoughtful, admiring and contemplative.

And me... As we exit the restaurant, I'm compiling a list of animals. I'm doing this in my head. I'm thinking about animals and how smart they are... For eating their young.

~~~ ★ ~~~

Parenting Survival Tip # 164: Hot wheels are bad for your health.

Have you ever... Placed one knee on your mattress, propelling yourself towards the pillow... Pulling back the covers as you go... Only to see something *large* and fast scurrying towards aforementioned knee... Causing you to back track *with haste*... losing your balance... Flailing... and nearly falling backwards out your unopened bedroom window... Only to remember that before dawn your son came to snuggle with you and left a Hot Wheel in the bed on your side.

Yeah. Me neither.

#BloodPressureis*Jacked*up
#NowINeedAScanForAneurysm
#IQuit

~~~ ★ ~~~

Parenting Survival Tip # 165. Teach them to encourage each other, and to try HARD to understand.

Upon further review of the story of the Christ child at bedtime:

Captain A: He was born where the animals sleep and eat and poop. And there was blood. And he had a belly corn. And that's gross.
B-Dubya: He had a what?

Captain A: A belly corn. (pointing to his tummy) I had one too. And Honey Badger had one... and the doctors pinched it shut.

Me: (recognition dawning) He means an umbilical cord B-Dubya. Everyone has them, even baby Jesus. Just nod and smile.

~~~ ★ ~~~

# Day 27

A memory from May 2014:

Last Friday...

I yelled ... At approximately 2:50 pm. I snapped. And I yelled. *A lot.*

Let me back up.

I was tired.

I was grumpy.

I was a mom.

I wanted a few minutes to myself. I needed to think. I had invited company over for dinner. And I hadn't begun cooking because I'm the chief of all procrastinators.

I was going to sneak out and grab some groceries. Going shopping alone is a mother's equivalent to sneaking off to a man cave, or going to the firing range. To go to a store alone... Incognito... Is almost like a trip to Maui. Almost.

And my daughter... wanted to come shopping with me.

Groaaaaaaan...

I wanted peace. That child . . .That beautiful girl, wanted to spend time with me. Truth be told, she had a dollar in her pocket, and she only wanted a Slim Jim. She didn't really want time with me. But rather, it was a means to an end... A dried beef jerky end.

At that moment... I was not a perfect mother.

Nevertheless, I overcame the urge to scream and run. I let her accompany me to the store.

And the child... She talked... And talked... And talked... And sang all the way to the store with me.

We shopped. She pushed the cart... The entire trip was spent dodging, weaving, placing herself into the line of danger, cutting people off.

The following is a summation of the whole trip:

Don't park there. Stay with me. Stay on this side. Stay on that side. Stay in the middle. Come over here. No so close. Stop it!!! That was my toe. Turn. Left. The other left. No, I'm not buying that. No, I'm not getting this even for your brother. Stop asking. Not going to happen. Don't hit her. Park here.

Check out.

I re-arrange cart. It's no easy task. This is Aldi, where they don't provide bags. And if you know me, you know I'm *not* buying bags. I have a ton of bags at home…..which I forgot to bring with me. I have one box, tons of fresh produce, and two dozen eggs.

The eggs… are important.

The eggs. . . are the reason I yelled.

Remember eggs.

We checked out. She tried to run over at *least* one more innocent pedestrian, and we finally made it to the car.

I stopped the cart on the edge of the sidewalk. B-Dubya was standing beside the cart to open her Slim Jim. Slim Jims are a treat in my house. They're important. They're amazing, and if you don't finish them before you walk in the door… You have to share them with *both* brothers. Slim Jims are coveted prizes. And that child was not missing out on *any* of her beef stick deliciousness.

So as she was opening her Slim Jim, I went to open my door.

As I got the door open, and turned to retrieve my cart of produce… I heard a sound.

It was a sound that would take my breath away… make me shudder and cringe.

It was the sound of a deep intake of daughter breath… followed by silence.

And then followed the silence (filled the gaping abyss where no twitch was heard) the sound of a grocery cart... full of tons of produce and a fresh cantaloupe... macaroni... and two dozen eggs... as it hit the pavement after it plummeted over the edge of the sidewalk.

It was the sound of an entire cart of groceries driving under the front bumper of my car, as my daughter was standing right beside the cart... opening a Slim Jim.

It was that sound.

Now I need to state clearly... At this point.

*I didn't yell.*

I picked up all the groceries from the ground. My daughter tried to help with the eggs. She ended up making a large mess... messier. I did it myself. I got all the groceries, minus about six eggs, into the car. I placed the eggs in last just to make sure they were secure. I breathed in deeply.

I asked B-Dubya to park the cart. She was busy with her Slim Jim. She didn't hear me.

I parked the cart myself, while muttering quietly about why God even gave me lungs and a voice to speak with since my children were *all* born without ears.

*Still* (blood pressure pumping) I didn't yell.

I looked behind me and both ways, and I placed the car in reverse.

It was at that moment that the momentum of my vehicle, propelled the cantaloupe that I just picked up off of the pavement... forward. It rolled off of the front seat... onto the top of the remaining eggs.

My nostrils flared and I sucked in half of the oxygen I need daily to breathe in one breath.

Still... I *didn't yell*.

I parked. Removed the cantaloupe. Rearranged the groceries... and made it onto the road without further incident.

Nonchalantly, from the backseat B-Dubya asked me, "Mom... What are you thinking right now?"

I wanted to be honest, but I didn't care to damage her ... Scar her for life. I didn't want to yell.

I replied honestly. "I'm thinking... I don't need to talk right now. I'm thinking I need to be quiet... and you need to turn on a movie." She happily complied.

We get home and I carried all the groceries into the house. B-Dubya was smart enough to know that at that point, I wanted nothing more than to be left alone with my wounded pride. . . My bruised avocado. . . And my broken eggs.

Captain A met me at the door. He was wearing blue jeans, no shirt, and a knit Elmo snow hat with hangy down ear cover things (Please keep in mind that he was wearing all of this and it was four thousand degrees outside, as we were in the middle of a Georgia summer).

Whatever... I *didn't yell.*

Then he spoke. "Mom... Are you in a bad mood?" It was incredibly clear that sister had come in and announced my misfortunes.

Deep breaths... No yelling. Nostrils flared slightly. I responded, "I don't know son... What did your sister tell you?"

He was so matter of fact, so carefree. "Yep... You're in a bad mood."

At that moment... I didn't yell. I only clearly stated. "Go. Away." It was *totally* for his physical safety.

He complied.

I proceeded to put groceries away. I finally took the time to really look over the damage. Then, I took an egg carton out of the fridge. It had one egg in it. I set that one solitary egg on the counter, and I rinsed the carton out. I gently rinsed off the surviving eggs from the cart catastrophe, and prepared to put all of my eggs into one carton.

In walks Captain A. He's the child who can't read facial expressions, he can't take note of physical signs of stresses and frustration. He hasn't yet mastered the art of reading and interpreting body language. This was made *very* clear to me when he opened his mouth and spoke, "Mom... What happened to all the eggs? Did you drop them on the ground momma? Did you break all the eggs? Did the cart fall under the car momma?"

*Deep* breaths... Lamaze style. I calmly responded through slightly clinched teeth, "I don't know son. What did your sister tell you?"

He ignored my question, but clearly stated, "Yep. You broke all the eggs."

*Still. . . I didn't yell.*

Instead, I wanted to give him the opportunity to help. He loves to be included in the kitchen, to feel like a big man. And even though my blood pressure was *pounding*, and my teeth were grinding, I desired to be a good mom. I was clearly trying.

Gently, I said, "Son... Please grab that egg off of the counter and gently bring it to me. It's only one. Be gentle son. Be careful not to break my last egg baby. Bring it to me."

He picked it up and walked across the kitchen. There was one last slot in the egg carton. This egg had a home.

The globe of the earth tilted on its axis somewhere between Captain A, the counter, and the egg carton. Physics changed, and all the rivers in the world began to flow backwards simultaneously. In slow motion, I heard him say, "Mom. Is it cracked? Is this one broken too? I want to crack it momma. Here, I'll help you."

At that moment. . . My child... My innocent, sweet, five-year-old amazing child. . . Took my egg... My last egg... And slammed it . . . Against the center of his Elmo covered his forehead. He then stood, in the center of my kitchen... Looking positively horrified and shocked that there is egg running down his face. There was yellow yolk dripping from the rim of his knit Elmo snow hat.

It was then that I began *to yell.*

And I yelled, and I yelled. I yelled some more. And then I finished my rant by telling him to go wash his hands with soap and water and stay out of my kitchen.

The child washed his hands, as I scrubbed egg off the floor.

Evidently the screams of a madwoman reached the back of our home and caused my husband to appear out of the back bedroom. I heard him ask why there was raw egg dripping off of our son's forehead and would he please go wash his face with soap and water.

Slowly, I calmed down. And then, I thought long and hard of my utter epic failure of a day. My groceries were bruised, my eggs broken, and my son. . .

At that moment, I was an epic failure as a momma.

Quietly, some verses came to my mind. Today, and I share them with you.

*I thank Christ Jesus our Lord, who has given me strength, that he considered me faithful, appointing me to his service. Even though I was once a blasphemer and a persecutor and a violent man, I was shown mercy because I acted in ignorance and unbelief. The grace of our Lord was poured out on me abundantly, along with the faith and love that are in Christ Jesus. Here is a trustworthy saying that deserves full acceptance: Christ Jesus came into the world to save sinners—of whom I am the worst.*

1 Timothy 1:12-15

Paul... The worst...

He never shied away from his past... Who he was. Where he came from...

And then David in Psalm 51. . . It's a beautiful honest recollection of his own brokenness. His imperfection.

David ... a man after God's own heart... Broken. "My sin is ever before me."

It occurred to me that as women, we have high expectations.

I'm a mother. I'm designed to love and nurture and care for and provide. It's my job to protect, to comfort. I was so embarrassed with myself in looking back. I yelled at my kid... Over an egg.

I yelled.

Then it crossed my mind that I shouldn't tell anyone that I yelled.

We, as women... We desire to put on a smile, and show no one our brokenness. We, as women, think that we should always have a snack ready and a story handy and a clean welcome mat. We, as women, think that all the cobwebs need to be swept away and our table appear sparkling, our floors mopped, our curtains dusted.

We feel as though we need to at least have the air of having it together because it's our *job* to hold down the fort and be the backbone... The glue.

*It's my job to be strong.*

But in my own strength, sometimes I forget that it isn't my perfection that draws people to Christ.

It's Christ himself.

It isn't my beauty or my dusted curtains... Or my fingerprint free glass... Or my mopped floors... Or my perfect children... *Pfffff ffffffffftttttttttttttt!*

Those things don't show people who Christ is.

Rather, it's Christ within me.

Christ shining through in my brokenness, my jagged edges and cracks.

My desperate need for grace. . .

My utter inability to get it right...

*That's* why I need Christ so desperately.

And that's what I long to convey.

I want to represent honestly, not with mock humility... Not airing out all the laundry for all the neighbors to gawk at... But a precious balance.

If we, as parents...As followers of Christ... If our priority is to have it all together, and all of our ducks must be in a perfect row, then we present that face to the world. We paint on a false face of perfection that's *completely* unattainable to other women and mothers, other dads and fellow believers. Worse yet, we will find ourselves painting portraits of perfection that are actually brushstrokes of deception to those who have no concept of who the Father is.

They'll only see a finished product when in all actuality, the Lord sees all of our cobwebs. No filters.

We need to be able to relate to the broken and to be honest about our brokenness and encourage each other to keep moving.

And in turn, we also need to learn that when we see the brokenness of others, we should help to hold them up. We can love them by sweeping up broken pieces and renewing their confidence, instead of whispering about it behind their backs and condemning them for sinning differently than we do.

We *all* need grace, *especially* in this world of parenting.

We have tough jobs. There are a *lot* of broken egg days behind some of us... And ahead of some of us.... We're all hopeful mommas... or daddies of one... and grandmamma of two... and then there's three... four... and more.

And none of us have the magic key to perfection. We only have air, opportunity and the grace of the Father, even though sometimes it feels like we're barely able to grasp the very hem of His garment.

Read this again as a reminder to have courage. Don't ever forget where you are. Don't lose sight of where you came from. Most importantly, on this chaotic daily grind, don't forget *Who* you belong to.

Go moms. Run the race dads. Cling tight to the shreds of your sanity. Go make a difference. Go out boldly women of the Most High. Encourage. Lift up. With every breath, glorify our faithful Father who doesn't yell. He doesn't write us off on our bad days. He doesn't get weary. He doesn't disown us, even when it's a hundred degrees outside, and we're wearing our brokenness, our scars, and our Elmo hats, with egg on our face.

~~~ ★ ~~~

Parenting Survival Tip # 166: Aim high, but remain practical.

Captain A just decided that for his fourth birthday, he wants to have a skiing party. I'm just gonna save y'all the trouble and have you meet us at the nearest ER. Thank you and good night.

~~~ ★ ~~~

Parenting Survival Tip # 3: Don't ask questions. You really *REALLY* don't want to know.

Captain A: (nonchalantly) Momma, I maybe ate a toenail before.
And maybe even a fingernail.

Me: (blink blink...blink blink) (slowly walking away) I don't
even want to know.

~~~ ★ ~~~

Parenting Survival Tip # 25: Always tell the truth.

B-Dubya: Momma, if I was an animal, what animal would I be?
Me: A horse.
B-Dubya: What animal would Captain A be?
Me: A panda.
Captain A: I'm a gorilla. (smoothly and with confidence) A
gorilla with karate moves.
Me: No. No... You'd be a Labrador puppy... With big feet.
Captain A: That's not fair!!!
Me: So, if you're a horse and Captain A is a puppy, what's your
youngest brother?
B-Dubya: (not missing a single beat) A honey badger.

Obviously...

~~~ ★ ~~~

Parenting Survival Tip # 52: Just smile and wave boys, smile and
wave.

They all probably have a hidden stash of hallucinogenics
somewhere... acid ... 'shrooms... something. You just haven't
found it yet.

The kids are playing. They have a friend over today.

B-Dubya: There are *entirely* too many elephants in this castle, Princess. You're grounded.

Maddie: I'm going for a walk.

Captain A: I have a Power Ranger credit card. It gives you powers. But if you take off your necklace, you die. Where's my sword?

What in the world just happened???

~~~ ★ ~~~

Parenting Survival Tip # 87: It doesn't make sense. But it does make for good stories.

Captain A: (focused) Devastating... Wow... That's really devastating... Hmmmm.... Devastating...

I turn my head to see my son "reading" one of his sister's book. Upside down of course.

Me: Is that interesting?

Captain A: (never looking up from the print. There are no pictures... just print) Yep.

Me: What does devastating mean son?

Captain A: It means weird. This book is *so* weird.

~~~ ★ ~~~

# Day 28

So, I've got a plethora of ridiculous things my husband and myself have had to say to our boys, and here's an abbreviated list:

Not happening. You don't need a snorkel to take a shower.

Quit licking the couch.

Who left the number 4 in my fridge?

Stop breathing on each other in public.

Yeah the ants are mad, wouldn't you be mad if a giant peed on your house?

Stop licking your brother.

Don't pee in the toilet at the same time, you'll end up peeing on each other.

Well that's what happens when you let people stand on your head.

No, Captain America doesn't need a bath.

Pee in the grass, not on people's tires.

Stop wearing the chair on your head.

You can't lick your hands clean. Go wash them... With soap.

Explain to me why you pooped in the yard instead of in the house.

Underwear aren't ninja masks. Neither are pull ups.

How did you *forget* that you cut your hair???

Yes. You have to wear shorts outside, we have neighbors.

Stop putting your rear on people.

Well if you hadn't thrown the frog, that wouldn't have happened.

Don't make the piggy banks fight.

Stop beating your brother with a minion.

Dude, you have got to stop getting naked at other people's houses.

Quit drawing rear ends on the door.

Get out of the bathroom. Take your egg with you.

We're done with this rave party. Put your light sabers away.

No, Michael Jackson didn't marry Lena Horn.

Penguins... Penguins live in Antartica. Not pagans. Read it again.

Take a moment and soak this information in. Re-read that list. Twice. And then remind yourself that you're *not* a failure as a person. Don't second guess yourself. It's not you. It's them.

~~~ ★ ~~~

Parenting Survival Tip # 41: You *must* grow a stomach of steel in order to do this thing successfully.

Mothering Boys 101: Can't get your son to touch asparagus for dinner?

Inform him politely that if he eats it... His body turns it into healthy wonderful foul smelling stench later in his belly (and beyond) It's like a revolting science experiment.

Plate clean. Captain A-0 Mommy-1

~~~ ★ ~~~

Parenting Survival Tip # 42: They'll pick it up. They'll repeat it.

Hanging out with new people makes your kid say interesting things. Honey Badger marched through my bedroom today and announced "Shabbat Shalom." He was marching through with a bamboo pole and only wearing a diaper. And I was all like: "May God's peace be on you too, but it's Monday dear."

So thankful for friendships that reach across denominational boundaries, loving my family enough to share Biblical heritage with us. We can take it now, and share it with other believers.

~~~ ★ ~~~

Parenting Survival Tip # 35: Remember that some trains of thought have no caboose.

One breath. No pause:

Is there such thing as a flying baby ant?
Did you know ants were really baby wasps?
Ants can climb high. They creep me out.
Did you know flies pee and poop on people? Have your ever seen that?
Would it hurt you if someone hit you in the stomach so hard that the whole earth shakes?
Would you be sad if I was dead? Because you wouldn't have somebody to play Boxcar children with?
When I'm a teenager, you're going to be an adult.

Musings from Captain A to his sister.

~~~ ★ ~~~

Parenting Survival Tip # 36: Sometimes, we all get tired.

Confessions of a tired mother:

I went in to pick up my sleeping five-year-old. The plan was to put him on the potty whilst he zzz's so that he wouldn't wet the bed. Hypothetically, I got distracted while I was lifting. He was sleeping soundly, and hovering face first about four inches off of his mattress. I got distracted by my daughter who let out a weird sleeping wheezing sound that reminded me of a sloppy spit filled balloon that was rapidly spinning around the room after being released. I was staring at her... Wondering what was wrong with my kids. My tired fingers slipped from under the sleeping boys arm pits. Unceremoniously, I dropped him on his lil' punkin' face. So, when he woke up and scrambled to a sitting position, I did what *any* good mother would do... I acted like it didn't happen. "Come on son. Wake up. We need to go potty." He shuffled to the bathroom looking confused. And now he's tucked back in.

Parenting at its finest.

~~~ ★ ~~~

# Day 29

So now, here we are at day twenty-nine. My intentions were thirty-one, but I'm tired... And I need a nap. This somehow seems the appropriate seems the appropriate place to stop. The best laid plans of mice and men and all that jazz.

The truth is, this book has been in the making for years. The intent has always been there. But indeed, life has a way of taking the best laid plans and slamming them against the concrete.

I've shared some of my favorite memories with this crazy family of mine. There is laughter here, always laughter.

But I must take a moment to be incredibly serious and honest. Honesty is probably my biggest strength and my biggest flaw all at the same time. One can be honest, and unintentionally display a family who appears to have it all together. One can be honest in their musings, and make it seem as though everything in their world is perfect.

You see, it's not the words that are penned, but those that aren't. The truth is also in the stories you don't see here on these pages.

Our family is held together with prayer and diligence. We're far from perfect, and while we love our children, we see them as real people. I love my husband, but there have been times he's caused me pain. I've sadly done the same to him. We're real, and we love life, but we too bleed red.

Our marriage has had its fair shares of heartbreaks and healings. We're a paycheck to paycheck family who would be nowhere and nothing were it not for the unmerited favor of the Lord. I've intentionally not used this book as a platform to push faith. I'm not a teacher. I'm not a prophet. I'm not a saint. Rather, I'm a mom. I'm an artist, a writer, a flawed wife.

And yet the Father has seen fit to allow me this opportunity to share some of our stories with the world. It's not because of who we are, but who He is. And He's good. And He's mighty. And He's holy. And He's so faithful, even when we fail. He is so very faithful.

There have been times over the past few years when we have felt like the rough waters of life were going to drown us all. We have faced foreclosure, disability, death of loved ones, and the brutality of mental illness within our families. We have cried. We have let things go. We have learned the value of loving hard when we have nothing else to hang onto. We hang on to our faith.

And I'd be remiss if I said that our faith was easy. It's quite the opposite. The harder we lean into the God of Abraham, Isaac and Jacob, the more it seems that the wind around this little house shakes and trembles. Every time we draw closer to Him, it's as though the fires of life get a little hotter. It's difficult. It's a battleground to be certain.

But still… Even as I write these words, and finish this final chapter of this book, I can't help but praise Him. We're not who we are as a family because our kids are funny, or because I have a knack for words. We didn't get here by accidently stumbling into the spotlight. Quite the contrary, we see each and every event in our lives as a God ordained moment to share truth. And that truth brings peace.

Our home is a beautiful mixture of chaos and peace, true divinely manufactured peace. He's building our family block by block. And we know that one day our kids will be able to look back and laugh, and sometimes cry at the things we've gone though. And one day, they'll have to choose whether to walk in our footsteps and get to know this incredible God… Or they'll grow and choose to go at life without the only ingredient that we hold that gives us hope. Him. Adonai. Elohim. The beginning and the end.

As we continue creating our stories, and growing and learning, my prayer is that each person who stumbles across these words will not only laugh, but be spurred to look for that one thing… That one thing that we *all* desire. Peace. And I want to take this final page to say that peace doesn't come in being successful. It comes in being faithful, and hiding in the shadow of the wings of a mighty, *mighty* Father who hears us when we cry out.

We will continue to walk out our faith the best way we know how, one day at a time… One memory to the next. And we will strive to continue to give Him all the glory for all that's good within us. If you don't know Him… You can. If you don't know how, I pray that you will find the words to call out to Him in prayer…

and then... When you're ready... Study. Study. *Study*... More and more and more... The key to everything I'm mentioning is not found in the words of church fathers, or religion... No. It's found in between the pages of the Bible. History proves that without my help. I'm convinced that the Father can draw anyone to Him, but only if that person is hungry.

Our family is a living testament that two unholy, broken people can be joined together and be used to minister. Our faith has recreated the people that we once were. And while this walk has been difficult, I'd never look back. I don't miss the woman I was before I encountered a holy God. And I love my husband now more than I ever did before he knelt before the Father.

Please search for Him. There is no other that can provide this peace... This joy... This. He's all we have and all we need.

And with that thought, I must go. Our youngest just fell asleep and Honey Badger needs some yogurt. And the saga continues.

Until next time...

Printed in the United States
By Bookmasters